Also by M. J. Harper

The History of Britain Revealed
available in the US as The Secret History of the English Language

The Megalithic Empire (with H L Vered)

A Megalithic Trade Route [lecture]
https://www.youtube.com/watch?v=VO6TFjNBJmU

The Distribution of Deserts [DVD]

A New Model of the Solar System [DVD]

Meetings with Remarkable
FORGERIES

M J Harper

Urquhart Press
urquhartpress@aol.com

Lightning Source (UK) Ltd
Chapter House, Pitfield
Kiln Farm, Milton Keynes MK11 3LW

http://www.lightningsource.com

Published by Urquhart Press 2017

A catalogue record for this book is available
from the British Library

ISBN 978-0-9542911-2-9

Set in Minion and Cambria

Chapter 1

Autumn Leaves

In September 2016 a book called *Meetings With Remarkable Manuscripts* by Dr Christopher de Hamel was published to rapturous acclaim. "It's the thriller of the millennium, one of the cultural highlights of the autumn," warbled Kirsty Wark on Newsnight. 'An endlessly fascinating and enjoyable book,' said the redoubtable Neil MacGregor. 'Full of delights,' agreed Tom Stoppard. 'De Hamel's book, scholarly but unfailingly readable, is the beginning of wisdom in all things scribal and scriptural,' summed up the Guardian.

You get the picture. The great and the good were lining up to pay tribute to this season's Big Thing. I don't usually concern myself with these passing enthusiasms, they're harmless enough, but when the British Intelligentsia start lionising academics it interferes with my long-term goal of getting the universities abolished. So on this occasion I shall have to put my foot down. These much admired manuscripts are for the most part forgeries. Most of history before about 1300 is forgery. After that it starts to be more a question of misinterpretation than bamboozlement. Sorting it all out is quite an undertaking but once you know what you're doing everything unravels quickly enough and what you are left with can be knitted back into shape with surprising ease.

This is true right across the academic board. We have reached the stage where all the donkey work has been done by the academics and it just remains for the rest of us, who don't make a living at it but now thanks to the internet have access to it, to take it all apart and build it all back. You would be amazed at how much tripe there is out there once you reflect that ever since the age of five you have been taking their word for it. Apart from a little bit of scientific method, it's all up for grabs.

In this book I will be dealing with a very small slice of the confection – a handful of sixth, seventh, eighth century gospel books. 'Dealing

1

with' meaning showing they are twelfth century forgeries made to look like sixth, seventh, eighth century gospel books. Ho hum, who cares, except maybe sixth, seventh, eighth century manuscript specialists? You should for a start because it doesn't really matter which bit of the problem you begin unpicking, the academics have spent so much time and effort – at our expense so don't waste your pity – weaving it all together that you can just follow the thread back out of the labyrinth. I think that's enough mixed metaphors but just one more thing. Once it starts to go it starts to go. It can get a bit hair-raising. So for now just concentrate on the small picture: if it looks like it came out of the Dark Age it won't have come out of the Dark Age, that's why it's called the Dark Age. Many of your most basic beliefs come out of the Dark Age.

*　　*　　*

A few ground rules you should be aware of. None of the manuscripts featured in this book have ever been scientifically dated. That might surprise you as nowadays this is a straightforward, cheap and non-destructive procedure. I can't offer you any science either – I've never clapped eyes on any of them – nor can I offer you any new scholarship – they wouldn't allow me a ticket to the British Library Reading Room (not if they've got any sense). But this hardly matters, it's all on the internet. In any case, neither science nor scholarship is required because the forgeries are so childish they wouldn't fool anyone who hasn't got some good reason for believing in them. Admittedly that would appear to include the entire world. This disconnect between myself and the world has been occurring rather a lot lately and is a worrying trend. The world wants to buck its ideas up if you want my opinion.

All quotes are from standard sources. They have been mildly cherry picked, occasionally concertinaed and sometimes lightly edited for comprehensibility so I haven't given chapter and verse, but they are uncontentious. Anything in bold is somebody else's work. I do specifically cite Dr de Hamel when using extracts from his book but these have had to be kept to a minimum due to Britain's ludicrously restrictive copyright laws. Not that Penguin Random House would risk the derision of silencing so obscure a critic on such footling grounds but you never can tell with behemoths. Let battle commence.

Chapter 2

The Gospels of St Augustine

D r de Hamel's book begins with a dramatic tableau

> **At the end of this chapter I will recount how Pope Benedict XVI and the Archbishop of Canterbury both bowed down before me, on live television, in front of the high altar of Westminster Abbey** [*Meetings with Remarkable Manuscripts*, p 10]

This is splendidly ironic. The whole book is written in a very engaging manner, full of scholarship yet quite free of academese. In other circumstances I would recommend it warmly. What brought these three luminaries together?

1) Dr de Hamel is the Librarian of Corpus Christi, Cambridge, and so the custodian of their most treasured possession, a book known as the *Gospels of St Augustine*, which he had brought to Westminster for the occasion
2) The book came to these shores in 597 AD with St Augustine and at the behest of Pope Gregory the Great, the most illustrious of Benedict XVI's predecessors
3) Saint Augustine founded Christianity in England and was the first Archbishop of Canterbury.

Big stakes indeed. So let us bow our heads for a few moments in silent prayer that the *Gospels of St Augustine* is all it's cracked up to be. Or in my case, that it isn't.

*　　*　　*

A golden rule of the forgery detection business is "The more remarkable an object, the more likely it is to be a forgery". One might forge Hitler's Diaries but not those of Mrs Enid Witherall, late of Hoe Street, Walthamstow. There is an exception to this rule because occasionally it is not the object itself that matters but something contained within it. For instance, suppose Enid's diaries had this entry

> **6th April**: Made will today. Used one of those forms off the internet. I've left everything to my nephew, Jimmy. He's always been a good boy. Unlike some I could mention. I've put it in a safe place where they won't find it.

If I were one of Enid's relatives (not Jimmy) I would be inclined to give that manuscript – for that is what hand-written documents are called – a thorough, not to say forensic, examination. The *Gospels of St Augustine* raises red flags under both the rule and the exception.

It is certainly one of the world's most remarkable manuscripts. Not just remarkable, it is *remarkably* remarkable. Actually it is remarkably *remarkably* remarkable because, if genuine, the Gospels of St Augustine has no less than three completely different claims to fame

1. It was the personal possession of the individual who introduced Christianity into England
2. It is the oldest non-archaeological artefact in England
3. It is the earliest manuscript anywhere in the world containing a written form of what would eventually become the world language, English

And yet, amidst all the fanfare, it has its Enid moments. Nestled between the Prologue and St Mark's Gospel there is just enough space for some future scribe to come along and copy in some distinctly unBiblical material. It is a will bequeathing a substantial property to the then current owners of the *Gospels*, St Augustine's Abbey in Canterbury. Another tip: if Enid's will had been lodged with her local solicitor and the will said she'd left a substantial property to that solicitor, the relatives (including Jimmy) might wish to have a word with the Law Society. This is what the scribe wrote on that blank page in the *Gospels of St Augustine*

> **Here it is declared in this document how Abbot Wulfric and Ealdred, son of the thegn Lyfing, came to an agreement about the estate at Cliffe. Through the fear of God and St Augustine and on the advice of his friends he commended himself and the estate to St Augustine's, and every year on St Augustine's day**

> he shall give a pound in token, and after his death the
> estate shall pass to St Augustine's, furnished as it is at
> that time. The witnesses of this are the community at
> St Augustine's and that at Christchurch, and Lyfing, his
> father, and Siweard and his brother Sired and Wulfstan
> of Saltwood and the other Wulfstan. And this is done
> forever without end on behalf of the souls of Siferth
> and his children. Amen.

Love that 'other Wulfstan'. It would seem the *Gospels of St Augustine* might be worth a thorough, not to say forensic, examination. Though I don't suppose the Law Society would take the case.

$$* \quad * \quad *$$

We begin, as is standard procedure when the authenticity of documents is in question, with provenance – the official history of the item under inspection from its origin to the present day. To be perfectly honest, the first four hundred years of the *Gospels of St Augustine* are decidedly murky, there being no record of its existence for those four hundred years. This is usually a big no-no when authenticating rare objects. Dr de Hamel was himself for many years a Sotheby's appraiser but he probably wasn't on duty when this memorable encounter occurred

> **Bloke with parcel:** I've got this Rembrandt here. What do
> you reckon it's worth?
> **Sotheby expert:** What is its provenance?
> **Bloke:** The first four hundred years are decidedly murky
> but it has been securely in my possession ever since I found
> it in a skip.
> **Sotheby expert:** Well, it could be extremely valuable, sir,
> we're going to have to take very good care of it. Gwendoline,
> would you ask security to come to the front desk.

Why then does Dr de Hamel – and the entirety of scholarly opinion – believe in the authenticity of the *Gospels of St Augustine*? They advance three lines of evidence. The first is the Venerable Bede who mentions that Pope Gregory sent a parcel of books to Canterbury in 601 to assist in the proselytising mission Augustine was heading up. Bede does not mention a gospel book but in any event this appears to contradict the notion of it being brought here by St Augustine. This is finessed in orthodox accounts

> **The manuscript is traditionally, and plausibly, considered to be either a volume brought by St Augustine to England with the Gregorian mission in 597, or one of a number of books recorded as being sent to him in 601 by Pope Gregory the Great – like other scholars, Kurt Weitzmann sees "no reason to doubt" the tradition**

The casual reader would be forgiven for not noticing they are admitting there is no historical evidence for the Gospels of St Augustine. The historians have used here the effective, if dangerous, 'either-or technique', one of the many 'finesses' that the use of *academese* allows.

Everybody thinks of academese as a meta-language conveying complex ideas in a neutral and objective way. A pain to read perhaps but necessary if emotional and other imprecisions of ordinary language are to avoided. It is nothing of the kind. It is a swindle perpetrated by academics on themselves, on their peer-reviewers and on their readers – though not directly on the general public who have to take their word for it, it being so painful to read. They just pay for it all. Perhaps they wouldn't if they knew that academese is obscuring the fact that the great majority of all academic writing is worthless (almost literally since these monographs, essays, papers, dissertations, theses and so forth are read on average by between one and two persons). So the general public does not know they consist overwhelmingly of un-evidenced commentary ('learned chat'), based either on disguised truisms or undisguised but unexamined assumptions. By rule, it is true, they must contain 'original material' but this is almost invariably a further example of something already and copiously established. They will frequently contain straightforward, if subliminally mendacious, tricks of the trade of the 'either-or' type. Believe me, when academics really have got something fresh and important to say they switch into very, very clear English.

Academese is always understated, advancing arguments in an endearingly tentative way that insists to the reader the writer is doing his best to show a lack of dogmatism, that the hypothesis being presented is somehow provisional and not to be understood as the last word on the subject, just the best that can be managed given 'what is known' and will soon no doubt be augmented, even replaced, by a better understanding of the situation at sometime in the future.

Modesty is a form of lying. In effect, the standard academic paper is not the last word, it is not the first word, it is the *only* word – and the writer has to provide a citation to that effect. His paper would be rejected were he saying something genuinely original because, by definition, there can be no citation for it. All this is disguised by academese. Were there ever a moratorium on academese, and all scholarly papers were obliged to be submitted in plain English, the vast majority would be rejected by peer reviewers on grounds of fatuity alone. The mendacity might show up too. But since this applies to the peer reviewers themselves when they come to write their own scholarly papers and peer-reviewed scholarly papers are the chief criterion for academic advancement, it ain't never gonna happen. If academese goes, the academics will go too. Shame. Nice people for the most part.

Let us see whether the 'either-or technique' will work for or against the Augustinian scholars. I'll throw in a bit of mock-algebra to provide some systems analysis in place of academese

1. x (the Gospels of St Augustine being at Canterbury c 600 AD) is important
2. x physically exists, can be inspected and scientifically dated at any time
3. y and z (Gregory's books) are not important
4. y and z do not physically exist and play no further part in the story
5. x has no historical evidence
6. y and z do have historical evidence (Bede mentions them)
7. x, y and z can be placed together using the either/or technique (they were all in Canterbury together c 600 AD)
8. x now has "no reason to doubt" status and further examination is neither necessary nor desirable

This is not only useful for establishing the bona fides of something important, it has useful knock-on effects for things that are even more important

7

9. though *y* and *z* are unimportant Bede is now strengthened as a source for important matters about which he is either a direct witness or an indirect but reliable reporter i.e. England 500 - 700 AD
10. Bede is the historical source for *a, b, c ... n* during that period
11. there is definitely "no reason to doubt" *a, b, c ... n*
12. *a, b, c ... n* is a complete skein of "no reason to doubt" facts about English history 500 - 700
13. the skein can be woven into a properly sourced and satisfying narrative history for England 500 - 700
14. England and its language 'English' was established in the period 500 - 700
15. the English and English-speakers now have a satisfying account of their own and their language's origins (something everyone devoutly wishes for, it's part of the human condition).

This is all very win-win and can last – it has lasted – for centuries but there is still that itsy-bitsy loosey-loosey thread, just about visible, sticking out of the woolly jumper. Technically, if you really wanted to nit-pick, there is still no historical evidence for *x*. What if somebody starts gently tugging at the loose thread and establishes *x* did not in fact happen? At first nothing changes. *X* may be important in itself but its disappearance does not change history in any way. Bede, for example, never even mentioned it so his status, if anything, is enhanced. To be perfectly honest, the removal of *x* could be a good thing – it just goes to show how historians are fully on the ball, quite unafraid to slaughter the most sacred of cows in their flinty-eyed pursuit of truth. Ah, but

16. *x* is now discarded
17. *y* and *z* have always been bracketed with *x*. It's in all the textbooks
18. *y* and *z* are a little bit discredited
19. Bede, responsible for *y* and *z*, may be a little bit discredited too
20. there might even be reason to doubt *a, b, c ... n*
21. the entire woolly jumper is in some danger of getting unravelled

22. a woolly jumper that has been keeping everybody warm for centuries
23. there are dark mutterings about those who might have been pulling the wool over everybody's eyes all this time
24. but then people start contemplating the biting winds of not having a satisfactory and satisfying history
25. given the choice between a doubtful history and staring into a history-less abyss, people go for the former (it's part of the human condition)
26. the loose thread gets tucked back in one way or another
27. still and all, it's an entertaining spectacle while it lasts. Watch and learn, watch and learn.

∗   ∗   ∗

The next strand of evidence put forward for the authenticity of the *Gospels of St Augustine* is

> **It was certainly in England by the late 7th or early 8th century when corrections and additions were made to the text in an insular hand**

'Insular' script is so-called because it is the characteristic style of the insular British Isles as opposed to how they do these things sur le continent

> **The main text is written in an Italian uncial hand which is widely accepted as dating to the 6th century – Rome or Monte Cassino have been suggested as the place of creation**

The problem here is both British *insular* and Italian *uncial* can be mastered by a competent calligrapher in a couple of days so claiming this as evidence is a bit like the bloke with the parcel saying, "Look, it's even been signed by Rembrandt." Nevertheless, if not exactly *diagnostic*, this is as far as it goes one for de Hamel and the forces of academe.

The third and main evidential justification is that while the gospel book itself can only be hazily dated, there are certain later additions ('marginalia' as they are called in the art trade) which provide a *terminus ante quem* (as it is called in the history trade) i.e. the latest date by which any given object must have come into existence. Marginalia cannot be written into a book unless the book already exists. The Abbot Wulfric bequest was one such 'marginalia' but there are eleven others, the earliest of which is on page seventy-five

> **Ealhburh grants a food-rent from land at Brabourne, Kent, to the community of St Augustine etc etc**

As this Ealhburh is known to have been flourishing in the mid-ninth century, the transaction can be securely dated and thus provides a mid-ninth century *terminus ante quem* for the book as a whole. There is though one slight complication – the entry was written into the book a hundred years later. As Dr de Hamel puts it

> **The earliest of these is copied in a tenth-century hand on to the page facing the prologue to Mark. It is the bequest in Old English of a woman called Ealhburh in the mid-ninth century granting to the abbey various pieces of produce from her property at Brabourne in Kent** [*Meetings*, p.27]

So a tenth-century rather than a ninth-century *terminus ante quem.* A minor point, certainly Dr de Hamel thinks so, but it does give the official provenance of the *Gospels of St Augustine* a curious timeline (dates rounded up)

AD 600 The book now known as the *Gospels of St Augustine* arrives in England

600 - 850 it is carefully preserved by Canterbury monks as a treasured object belonging to or closely associated with the founder of their community and indeed of English Christianity

850 a woman gives some agricultural produce to these monks in exchange for the monks singing Psalm XX every day on her behalf. This agreement was recorded by means unknown

850 - 950 book continues to be carefully preserved by the Canterbury monks

950 the monks decide to deface their most treasured possession in order to record a transaction concerning agricultural produce and psalm singing made a hundred years before and which can have no significance now the woman is long gone but it does *en passant* confirm St Augustine's Abbey is the legal owner of some property at Brabourne in Kent. Should anyone ask.

Ninth century, tenth century, what does it matter? But speaking of defacement, the first few pages of the treasured book are missing. Not quite treasured enough. As Dr de Hamel tells us

> **The manuscript opens mid-word in the *capitula* list preceding the Gospel of St Matthew** [*Meetings*, p.19]

Although de Hamel and his colleagues treat missing opening pages as just normal wear and tear for ancient manuscripts, this runs foul of another of our golden rules: "Opening out, forgers about." The reason is that *text* is easy to reproduce but *introductions* are not. Anyone can turn out a Gospel of St Matthew but title pages, frontispieces, notes regarding who/where/when/why the book was made, the original owner's scribbled name on the flyleaf are all potential pitfalls for the forger. So forgers do their best to ensure opening pages are missing whenever possible. This stratagem never arouses suspicion because the authenticators of ancient manuscripts always treat missing pages as just normal wear and tear.

These are not the only pages that have gone dubiously walkabout. Most early gospel books were profusely illustrated and the *Gospels of St Augustine* is no different. However, few of the original pictures in the book have 'come down to us', as the phrase has it, but those that have survived are useful for establishing its true provenance. Dr de Hamel for one finds them helpful

> **The inclusion of integral pictures, even if only two now survive, is of importance too in assigning the manuscript to an origin under the patronage of Gregory the Great, since Gregory himself made a famous defence of the value of religious illustrations**
> [*Meetings*, p.39]

11

and who are we to disagree since one of the illustrations is a blatant smoking gun left by the forgers. Twelfth century forgers were highly professional craftsmen but not trained in art history. Like all art forgers, they could reproduce pictures of any period so long as they had the originals to work from. As there were no illustrated gospel books from the sixth century – or at least they didn't have access to any of them – they simply used twelfth century styles and made them coarser, more rustic, less polished, to reflect that artists of five hundred years earlier would, in all probability, be *like* them but not as *advanced* as them. This simple ruse has fooled generations of modern scholars who *are* trained in art history but think there is nothing unusual in styles hanging around for half a millennium. If they do come across glaring anachronisms of this sort they have no difficulty explaining them away. Here is de Hamel's caption for one of the St Augustine illustrations

> **The picture of the Last Supper in the Gospels of Saint Augustine was copied nearly five hundred years later into the Bayeux Tapestry, where it was adapted to become the scene of Odo of Bayeux feasting with his nobles** [*Meetings*, p.48]

It would appear the dear ladies embroidering the Bayeux Tapestry had a conversation something along these lines:

"What's next on the list, Doris?"
"Odo feast scene, Marge. What do you reckon?"
"Dunno, how about a Last Supper type of treatment. You
  know, with Odo taking the place of Christ?"
"That's pushing it a bit, isn't it?"
"His lot are paying."
"Fair point. What have we got for Last Suppers?"
"There's that one in the Augustinian Gospels. We could use
  that."
"Leave it out, dear, that's five hundred years old!"
"Form is temporary, Doris, class is permanent."

Bayeux might seem a long way from Canterbury but as it happens – and it says a lot about the opacity of medieval history – nobody knows where the Bayeux Tapestry was in fact made, though Dr de Hamel has a theory

The Gospel Book of Saint Augustine therefore has a part to play in the argument that the Bayeux Tapestry was actually made in Canterbury [*Meetings*, p.47]

✶　✶　✶

We turn next to the 'marginalia'. The official line is we are dealing with a standard early gospel book consisting of Matthew, Mark, Luke and John, with some accompanying lists and commentaries, all written in Latin in Italy during the sixth century. After it arrived in England, English hands got to work on it. In the seventh century some minor erasures and alterations to the text were made (in Latin) for reasons that are obscure, but in the tenth century the monks of St Augustine's Abbey, founded by the great man himself, started using blank pages in his gospel book to record documents of importance to their abbey. These additions, mainly in Anglo-Saxon, consist of eleven land charters and one list of relics held by the abbey. Land holdings and relics could be thought strange bedfellows but most medieval monastic foundations relied on two income streams: rents from land and offerings from pilgrims come to see the relics. Before Becketomania took over in the thirteenth century, the abbey's relics were the main draw in Canterbury, England's premier visitor destination. St Augustine's Abbey, Canterbury, and Canterbury Cathedral were something of a joint operation.

Quite why the abbey thought it necessary to list their relics in the *Gospels of St Augustine* is baffling but the relics themselves provide an insight into Canterbury's attitude to authenticity in general. Most of them are routine – crumbs of the true cross, pieces of the Virgin Mary's cloak, hair of St Cecilia – but very appropriately they also had a finger of Pope Gregory, presumably included in a later package from Rome than the parcel of books he sent over. There was an arm of St Bartholomew but, not wishing to be unkind, apostles' arms are two a penny in the pilgrimage trade; the abbey's real pride and joy was the head of the beheaded (in 316 AD) St Blaise. St Blaise has always been one of the most popular of all the patron saints – sore throats, wild animals, the wool trade – so getting the head was a coup. Everybody else had to make do with the off-cuts. Come to think of it, the relics probably do merit their place in the Augustine Gospels.

Ironically the relationship between medieval pilgrims and their relics is mirrored by the relationship between modern historians and Anglo-Saxon land charters. They want to believe in them, they demand evidence as to why they should believe in them, they proceed on the basis they do believe in them ... but there are always those nagging doubts. Which may not always be shared with the lay audience so here's a fun quiz you can try at home. Study this passage from an accredited authority

> Over a thousand Anglo-Saxon charters are extant today,
> as a result of being maintained in the archives of religious
> houses. These preserved their charters so as to record their
> right to land. Some surviving charters are later copies

Obviously the *original* charters are historical gold, being contemporary witness to what was actually going on in Anglo-Saxon England. The copies, less so. What you have to do is consider the phrase 'some surviving charters' in the above passage and estimate the kind of number the writer is trying to convey. Is it

a) half-a-dozen, a dozen, maybe a few more
b) fifty or thereabouts
c) could it be a hundred, even two hundred?

The correct answer is d) eight hundred

> Overall, some two hundred charters exist in the
> original form whilst others are post-Conquest copies

We cannot say (I mean, modern historians cannot say) whether the copies are genuine or not, so let us concentrate on the two hundred claimed to be originals, and therefore presumed genuine. As usual with such fine judgements, it all boils down to a battle of wits between forgers and authenticators. So, Question Two in your home quiz

> *There are two hundred Anglo-Saxon land charters whose*
> *authenticity will be decided by one of two groups, forgers*
> *and authenticators. Using your skill and judgement, which*
> *of the two groups do you think will prevail?*

1. Professional forgers whose fulltime job is the creation of authentic-seeming Anglo-Saxon land charters and all the

necessary appurtenances. Their work has to withstand the scrutiny of legal, albeit medieval, authorities

2. Professional historians whose fulltime job is lecturing and writing about Anglo-Saxon England. Their jobs would be at risk were there no authentic Anglo-Saxon land charters and all the necessary appurtenances. Their work has to withstand the peer review of other professional historians whose fulltime job is lecturing and writing about Anglo-Saxon England.

None of this bears directly on the authenticity of the *Gospels of St Augustine*. Even if every single Anglo-Saxon land charter in it were bogus this would not prove the gospel book itself is bogus. If the book was truly written in Italy during the sixth century it could still be a repository for land charters, genuine or otherwise, written in England during the tenth, eleventh and twelfth centuries. *Unless there was some reason why these particular charters needed to be associated with St Augustine and his gospel book.* That would be mighty fishy. Let us, so to speak, forge that link. To do this we shall need to look at the orthodox history of land tenure in England. It will be mercifully short and dates will once again be occasionally rounded up

pre-AD 43 nothing known

43 - 400 England is part of the Roman Empire. All land is held at the whim of the Roman authorities. No information about how land was apportioned, title to land established, ownership recorded etc.

400 - 500 Romans leave, nothing known, everything 'in flux'

500 - 900 Anglo-Saxon kingdoms are established throughout England. Land appears to be distributed among and by Anglo-Saxon kings, thegns, monasteries, commoners etc. The title to that land is verified in a number of ways – mainly customary rights and force but also, reportedly, written land charters

15

900 - 1066 Another period of flux as Anglo-Saxon and Danish regimes vie for supremacy. Since some kind of legitimacy is continuous, land holdings too are continuous but 'subject to change'

1066 Norman Conquest. Ownership of all English land is vested in William the Conqueror

1066 -1139 Feudal system. Technically all land is owned by the king and large parts continue to be owned directly by the king, but most is given to Norman magnates and others who assisted in the original Conquest, and they in turn parcel land out to people useful to *them* e.g. men-at-arms, the Church, monasteries, tenant farmers etc. Often new people, sometimes the previous people. Not everyone was given formal written title to specific areas of land. If, for instance, a magnate's job was to guard the Welsh border he might be given, say, 'the land and entitlements of Shrewsbury' but what that amounted to would be largely a matter of what he could hold and keep, not just vis à vis the Welsh but vis à vis other Norman magnates on either side. What he ended up with may or may not be formally recorded but either way it was 'subject to change' depending on his relationship with the central Norman authorities in London. On the other hand these same authorities, including Norman law courts such as they were, could be expected to support him in his peaceable and heritable (for a price) land holdings.

1139 - 1153 Civil War between King Stephen, representing the existing Norman administration, and Empress Matilda, representing the potentially new Angevin regime. Land ownership is not necessarily underwritten and enforced by the central authorities because a) there was not much by way of a central authority during the civil wars and b) it might turn out to be the wrong central authority.

1153 Angevins win. All landowners have reason to seek some kind of legitimacy for their ownership over and above any arrangements entered into during the previous Norman administration. The Angevins prove to be a strong central authority and, to make that authority a reality on the ground, established much more effective law courts. In the way of all law courts, these were particularly cognisant of legal documentation so in disputes over land ownership, charters could be decisive. Unfortunately, at this stage of English history, land charters were a) thin on the ground and b) possibly associated with the now tainted Norman regime. Fortuitously, charters *predating* the Norman regime, i.e. from the Anglo-Saxon period, start turning up in great numbers!

The Church and the monastic houses were large landowners and had a monopoly over all writing, including land charters. In addition the canon lawyers staffing the new courts were themselves obliged to be in holy orders. Not surprisingly the ecclesiastical sector were enthusiasts for this new world order of due process, and often came to court armed with one of these 'Anglo-Saxon' land charters. Even so it required adroit handling, as instanced by one of the 'Anglo-Saxon' charters in the *Gospels of St Augustine*, dealing with ownership of Plumstead, a Kentish manor near the Thames estuary. The subsequent shenanigans are the stuff of modern history

> **Charter regarding land at Plumstead, S809. Latin with Old English. A.D. 961 x 971 (? 963). King Edgar to St Augustine's Abbey, Canterbury; grant of 4 sulungs (*aratra*) at Plumstead, Kent**

But not for long

> **The manor was given, in 960, by King Edgar, to Canterbury abbey; went, for a time, to Earl Godwin's son Tostan, and to Bishop Odo**

The famous Bishop Odo

> Little good is recorded of Odo, and it was recorded that
> his vast wealth was gained by extortion and robbery.
> His ambitions were boundless and his morals lax

As the people doing the recording were church scribes and church property was frequently what Odo most coveted, it is little wonder if no good was recorded about him. They may have had a point

> In 1076 at the Trial of Penenden Heath Odo was
> tried in front of a large and senior assembly over the
> course of three days at Penenden Heath in Kent for
> defrauding the Crown and the Diocese of Canterbury.
> At the conclusion of the trial he was forced to return
> a number of properties and his assets were re-
> apportioned

Before Odo could fight back

> In 1082, Odo was suddenly disgraced and imprisoned
> for having planned a military expedition to Italy. His
> motivations are not certain. Chroniclers writing a
> generation later said Odo desired to make himself Pope
> during the Investiture Controversy while Pope Gregory
> VII was in severe difficulty in his conflict with Henry
> IV, Holy Roman Emperor, and the position of Pope
> was in contention, but the contemporary evidence is
> ambiguous. Whatever the reason, Odo spent the next
> five years in prison, and his English estates were taken
> back by the king, as was his office as Earl of Kent. Odo
> was not deposed as Bishop of Bayeux

Things were looking good for the Canterbury interest and it was thought meet to include the ownership of Plumstead in the Domesday Book. But, in the circumstances, better not mention Odo

> Property is recorded in Domesday Book 2.25 sulungs
> Plumstead. There are two entries which say Plumstead
> belonged to Brictsi the noble in 1066, in 1086 it was
> held by St Augustine's Canterbury, the second entry
> says Surag in 1066, St Augustine's in 1086

But Canterbury was by no means out of the woods

> On his deathbed in 1087, William I [the Conqueror]
> was reluctantly persuaded by his half-brother, Robert,

Count of Mortain, to release Odo. After the king's death, Odo returned to England. William's eldest son, Robert Curthose, had been made duke of Normandy, while Robert's brother, William Rufus, had received the throne of England. Odo supported Robert Curthose's claim to England. The Rebellion of 1088 failed and William Rufus permitted Odo to leave the kingdom. Afterwards, Odo remained in the service of Robert in Normandy

Even our normally credulous historians have concluded the ever so convenient 'Anglo-Saxon' charter in the Gospels of St Augustine was a forgery

Comments: Turner 1915, pp. xxxii-iii; Kelly, *St Augustine's*, pp. 113-15, fabrication, probably of 11th century, modelled on 9th-century charter (perhaps S 332)

It says something about the precariousness of land tenure at this period that the largest monastic order (the Benedictines), with the backing of the most powerful prelate (the Archbishop of Canterbury), owning land recorded in the most authoritative property register (the Domesday Book) should *still* think it necessary to fabricate an Anglo-Saxon land charter. Just in case.

But again, this does not bear directly on the authenticity of the *Gospels of St Augustine*. Yes, Augustine's great antiquity might be useful against a nouveau character like Odo but why would the Canterbury monks think it necessary to come up with a very old book to record what were, after all, relatively recent land dealings? Were they maybe worried about competing claims from certain persons with more ancient pedigrees than Norman conquistadors? Let us find out.

The Rule of Law in the twelfth century was not as it is today; ownership of land was decided more by force than by judicial fiat. The Church was a landowner on a vast scale but it did not have access to much *force*, land charters would not deter anybody who did. There was though one circumstance in which land charters might deter would-be despoilers. Being a landowner on a vast scale meant the Church itself could end up being both plaintiff and defendant. It might be thought unusual, faintly irreligious, for the Church to find itself in such unseemly imbroglios but these intramural disputes were in fact a staple of court proceedings in the high Middle Ages, and were often decided by evidence as to who owned what, when and under whose auspices. What did the relevant land charter say? Great care needed to be taken; all sides knew very well land charters were in short supply and not perhaps always to be trusted. Proceedings could easily slip into Justice Cocklecarrot territory

> Might I direct Your Honour's attention to his honour's Bundle A marked "Cartulary of Land Charters of the reign of Cynewulf and Appurtenances" where it will be immediately apparent to Your Honour that our forged land charter clearly predates the plaintiff's forged land charter and therefore I respectfully request a swift disposition of this frivolous and, I might venture to suggest, opportunist claim

The Plumstead estate illustrates why these cases arose and how they were handled. Plumstead is geographically part of the see (bishopric) of Rochester and is some distance from the see of Canterbury. Contrariwise Rochester had acquired extensive holdings in the Weald and along the Channel coast, within the purlieu of Canterbury. A recipe for discord and, while Canterbury monks were dab hands at coming up with Anglo-Saxon land charters, Rochester was just as dab

> **Thirty-three Saxon charters are known for Rochester. Four, dating from AD 604 to AD 868, are of particular significance ... the foundation charter of the church and priory, AD 604; a land grant from Aethelbert, King of Kent, to the church of St Andrew and St Justus, its first bishop ... The rest record grants of land and grazing or pasture rights to the bishop, church and priory**

Neighbourly disputes between Canterbury and Rochester could take various forms

> **After Gueleran's death in 1184 a great dispute arose between the monks of Canterbury and Rochester, concerning the placing of the pastoral staff of the deceased bishop on the altar of Christ church, to be left there, and delivered by the former to the new bishop,**

20

but on the interposition of the archbishop, the latter at last acquiesced, and the whole of this ceremony was performed accordingly

What was it really about?

> In 1185, they elected Gilbert de Glanvill, who soon after his coming to the see, demanded from them many of the manors and possessions which his predecessor, bishop Gundulph, had given to them, which he alleged had belonged to his see, which was greatly impoverished by his granting them away from it. This occasioned a dispute, which was carried on with uncommon heat and violence for some years; but the monks were in the end obliged to submit to his clemency, and award in everything they had contested with him, and the bishop again resumed several of the manors and possessions above mentioned for the maintenance of himself and his successors. The monks were put to such heavy charges during this litigation, that they were necessitated to coin the silver shrine of St. Paulinus into money

You've got to bet some to get some. The different branches of the Church, monasteries as well as bishoprics, were large landlords but they often had to pay if they wanted to stay large landlords.

Canterbury was certainly prepared to pay for the creation of the *Gospels of St Augustine*. But why did they go to the bother of going back to the very earliest days long before the land charters they were dealing with? The answer is their chief rival, Rochester, could claim to have *nearly* as ancient a pedigree

In Augustine's day, there were already two bishoprics for Kent, Canterbury and Rochester

What Canterbury had that Rochester did not was, of course, St Augustine himself and he being the earliest Christian in England, his gospel book will by definition be the earliest gospel book in England. That gives Canterbury the scope for writing in charters earlier than Rochester, so the purported date of *any* land charter will be whatever is required to win any particular dispute. Rochester used the exact same strategy

> ... in AD 604 Aethelbert of Kent gave the south-western
> quarter of the town for the foundation of the church
> (later the cathedral) and priory of St Andrew

This is in a cartulary called the *Textus Roffensis* [Roffensis = of Rochester] compiled in the twelfth century and if you believe a manuscript written in 604 will still be around in 1175 in order to be copied into a cartulary, you'll believe anything. Rochester's official historian does not believe it though he cannot quite admit it in so many words

> Eardulf seems to have been consecrated bishop of
> this see soon after 747 AD during whose government
> here the church of Rochester may be said to have
> recovered in some measure its past misfortunes, by the
> countenance and assistance of several princes, though
> there appears to be great confusion in the dates of the
> several grants made to it

You bet there was. Confusion about the dates was the least of their worries

> Godwyn I was at the council at Kingsbury, in 851.
> From this period to the Norman conquest the account
> of the bishops of this see is mutilated and uncertain.
> The deplorable state of those times, occasioned by the
> confusion of the Danish wars, darkening the history of
> both church and state with impenetrable obscurity; so
> far indeed we know by what followed, that most of the
> estates of this church were wrested from it, by one side or
> the other, none of which seem to have been restored till
> after the Norman conquest, so that this church and its
> bishops must have continued in a state of great poverty
> till that time

Not so poor they could not manage to preserve for five hundred years the *original charter* as given to them by King Aethelbert. We know this because they copied it into the Textus Roffensis and the Textus Roffensis has survived. Which is more than can be said for the original charter. The funny thing is, we can have copies, we can have what are claimed to be originals, but it seems we can never have both copies *and* originals. This affords an insight into historians' notions about medieval record keeping

"Quick, copy it into that cartulary before the next wave of foreigners comes along."

"Shall I destroy the original?"

"Yes, yes! Of course destroy the original. You've been here long enough to know that."

"I thought just this once ... it's King Aethelbert himself ..."

"You're not here to think. It's tradition. You don't mess with tradition. You know the rule as well as I do: take care of the copy as if your life depended on it, destroy the original."

∗   ∗   ∗

The *Gospels of St Augustine* had those three remarkable properties

1. It was the personal possession of the individual who introduced Christianity to England
2. It is the oldest non-archaeological artefact in England
3. It is the earliest manuscript containing a written form of the language which would eventually become the world language, English.

We can now account for two of these. The twelfth century Canterbury monks created this gospel book *precisely* because its purported owner introduced Christianity into England and can therefore be associated with the very earliest Church documents. In doing this the monks unintentionally created what modern historians have taken to be England's oldest non-archaeological artefact. Historians have been equally bamboozled by the third particularity of the Gospels of St Augustine, the Anglo-Saxon writing in it. They do not even ask themselves *why* there is Anglo-Saxon writing in it. After all, most legal documents, even in Anglo-Saxon times, were written in Latin and continued to be so for many centuries after the Anglo-Saxon period. The historians' blunder is serious because why certain documents were written in Anglo-Saxon and *when they were written* affects not just the authenticity of this or that gospel book, not just the authenticity of this or that land charter, it affects the authenticity of English history.

According to de Hamel and everybody else, the earliest book containing English writing is the *Gospels of St Augustine*. They are not claiming the writing in it is the earliest example we have of written English. These same scholars believe the Anglo-Saxon sections in it, the charters, are relatively late, ninth- or tenth-century. But whenever these charters were written, none of the scholars have mused why they are in Anglo-Saxon and not in Latin. Let us muse for them. The explanation is simple enough and arises from an inherent shortcoming of the Latin language.

It is all very well using Latin for *important* stuff such as state papers, diplomatic correspondence, national histories, monumental inscriptions, the Bible, because everything they contain is important and hence familiar. Latin deals admirably with such material irrespective of what language any of it was couched in originally. The people and places being recorded are so recognisable that, however they are expressed in Latin, everybody knows exactly who or what is being referred to. But what about this, the purportedly earliest dated land charter in England?

> A charter of Aethelraed I AD 868, granting the north-west quarter to Cuthwulf, bishop of Rochester, 'here are the boundaries as far as the Mead Way from Doddinghyrnan west along the Street out to the wall, and so by northern way out to Liabingescot (Liaba's house) ... to where the wall turns east, and so east within the wall to the Great Gate over against Doddinghurnan, then straight south from the gate ... to Doddinghurnan'

It is not so straightforward. True, by employing various arbitrary transliterations, a Latin-trained scribe could invent credible Latin versions for all these people and places but unfortunately, when that land charter is required for its sole purpose – to demonstrate unequivocally who owns what, who authorised it and who witnessed it – that scribe will not be around to specify who or what he was referring to. It would be open to anybody to argue the charter in fact referred to quite different people, in quite different places. Not the best title deed one could hope for. Much better to write it in the everyday language of the people and places, then there can be no dispute. The Medway Council Archives, the present custodians of this particular charter, pronounce with understandable pride

> If the boundary clause is indeed very ancient, this document contains the first record of place

24

> names or street names in the English language ...
> The Street is Watling Street i.e. Rochester High
> Street; Doddinghern [Lane] is now Boley Hill
> (formerly King's Head Lane) ...

Though local pride does not overrule scholarly rectitude

> **However, the document is in part at least a later
> forgery in common with many charters of the Anglo-
> Saxon period and was devised to give legal basis to
> rights not otherwise recorded**

Exactly so. Although all scribes were Latin-trained and, for the most part, wrote Latin documents intended to be read by other Latin-trained scribes, land charters were written in English, and land charters have a distressing tendency to be 'later forgeries'. This creates a severe problem for the authenticity of the *Gospels of St Augustine*. The chief reason de Hamel and his confrères claim the book must be ancient was that the Ealhburg prayers-for-produce bequest of the ninth century provided a *terminus ante quem*. If all charters written in Anglo-Saxon may or may not be later forgeries, each one has to be examined on its merits, but since everyone acknowledges the charters in the Gospels of St Augustine are copies anyway, *they cannot be examined on their merits*. The authenticity of original documents can be established by various means but the authenticity of copies has to rely on the good faith of the copyist. And one thing all scholars agree is that medieval land charter 'copyists' are not to be counted on to act in good faith.

The whole basis of the Gospels of St Augustine being from the Anglo-Saxon period *at all* has now fallen away. It still might be, there is just no reliable evidence it was. This is bad enough as regards the narrow question of whether the *Gospels of St Augustine* is genuine but what is much, much worse is that St Augustine himself is central to our understanding of how the Anglo-Saxon language came to be written down. As this is a fundamental cornerstone of English history, it unavoidably becomes a matter demanding investigation. It does not stand up to investigation.

*   *   *

When *was* Anglo-Saxon first written down? When, as the philologists would put it, did this vernacular tongue become a literary language? Converting speech into an alphabetic written form is a tremendously arduous and complex business. So arduous and so complex that generally speaking it is done once and once only for any given language. However well or badly the job is done, a QWERTY situation arises and it is better to put up with an inefficient system than have everyone retrain using something more logical. English is a bit of a curiosity. It was done twice! Once, we are told, in the sixth century using an Anglo-Saxon alphabet, Latin plus a few Anglo-Saxon letters, then again many hundreds of years later, using the Latin alphabet plus a few English letters.

The situation is thoroughly confusing because everybody is relying on later copies but we can all agree rendering *spoken* Anglo-Saxon into *written* Anglo-Saxon was a formidable task at any time and doubly so in the uncouth turbulence of the sixth century. Exceptional too, considering the last European language rendered into alphabetic form was Latin itself some thousand years before. Going by the textbook version of history, everyone had been contentedly using Latin to write things down, when suddenly out of the gloom the Anglo-Saxons emerged. A thousand years was too long, they decided, what the world needed was a new written language! But when *exactly* is this extraordinary development in European culture supposed to have happened? What, in other words, is the *terminus ante quem* of written Anglo-Saxon?

> **The Law of Æthelberht is a set of legal provisions written in Old English [i.e. Anglo-Saxon], probably dating to the 590's or early 7th century. It originates in the kingdom of Kent, and is the first Germanic language law code. It is also thought to be the earliest example of a document written in English**

So Anglo-Saxon officially had become a written language *by* c 600 but a terminus ante quem does not tell us *when* it happened. However, we do know *where* this momentous development occurred thanks to another Amazing Fact They Never Told You. Anglo-Saxon is the sole language on record written abroad but unwritten in its homeland. We have a vast array of documents written in Anglo-Saxon emanating from England, but not a single one emanating from the Anglo-Saxon homeland. Since historians, linguists and ethnologists rely so much on written sources, we are still waiting to find out where that homeland was! Written Anglo-Saxon, then, must be an English invention, invented in England. But when, where and by whom in England?

We know a fair bit about the early Anglo-Saxon period in England because a native, i.e. not Anglo-Saxon, monk called Gildas [*fl.* 500–570] thoughtfully wrote a pretty full account of it and lots of other people were thoughtful enough to copy it and copy it and copy it until you can get your own copy of Gildas from the library. The Anglo-Saxons, it seemed, arrived in 495 and then spent the following hundred years conquering England, settling England and establishing reasonably permanent kingdoms to govern England. Not perhaps the most propitious century to be doing what for a millennium nobody else had been able to do nor shown much interest in doing – the rendering of one's own spoken tongue into an alphabetic literary language. Gildas, for one, did not rate Anglo-Saxon cultural proclivities highly – very much the reverse – and certainly made no reference to any literary interests and capabilities. Yet somehow modern historians have to explain

The Law of Æthelberht ... dating to the 590's or early 7th century ... is thought to be the earliest example of a document written in English

This makes no sense. Academics do everything to avoid situations that make no sense. Intellectual curiosity was what they had when they were undergraduates, it is not appropriate for grown-ups. They tend to take things as they find them, in other words the prevailing orthodoxy, whether it makes sense or not. They would be thrown out on their ear if they didn't. Academic historians go one step further: they *must* take things as they find them – they are trained to identify, interpret and comment on the 'extant contemporaneous written record', in other words things that have already been found. There is a reason for this professional self-effacement. Before academic history, there was just *history* and since that was always shamelessly 'political', its present practitioners follow the dictum if it isn't in the extant contemporaneous written record, it isn't proper history. They are discouraged, if not downright forbidden, from speculating too much about things *not* in the written record. So if neither Gildas nor the Anglo-Saxons

27

themselves left an account of how 'English' became a literary language, it is not for historians to make it up. This originally benevolent self-denying ordinance now paralyses the whole study of history. Let us start breathing life into the palsied corpus. There would appear to be three possibilities to account for Early Written English:

1. It was a domestic development. The English branch of the Anglo-Saxons undertook the phenomenal task of creating Europe's first literary language for a thousand years. We do not know how or why this came about. *This explanation, however unlikely, is tacitly the current default assumption among professional practitioners.*

2. St Augustine, or the cultural forces he spearheaded, kick-started the process. This would be odd because the cultural forces St Augustine spearheaded, a.k.a. the Catholic Church, made strenuous efforts to ensure Latin was the *only* literary language for the next thousand years (cf. the Roman Empire doing much the same for the preceding thousand years). Encouraging the locals to break this priceless monopoly would be perverse in the extreme. *This explanation, though equally unlikely, does have the merit of providing some kind of coherent narrative, and is sometimes provisionally put forward by professional practitioners.*

3. It never happened. The 'extant contemporaneous written record' purporting to demonstrate it did, i.e. sixth/seventh century documents written in Anglo-Saxon, are forgeries. *This explanation has not been considered by professional practitioners.*

We cannot re-run the first scenario, 'nothing is known', but the second one is more promising because 'a coherent narrative' has been put together from various not-quite contemporaneous sources. From these we can reconstruct that momentous event in English history, when Augustine met Aethelberht

Aethelberht: Welcome, Augustine, what can I do for you?
Augustine: Would you like to convert to Christianity?
Aethelberht: I'm open to offers. The wife's a Christian, you know. Well, of course you would know, you must have stayed with her father, Charibert King of the Franks, on your way through.
Augustine: Yes indeed, he sends his regards. If you do convert,

you'll be saved from eternal damnation in the pits of hell.

Aethelberht: That's always useful but I was thinking of something more *here and now*.

Augustine: I can bestow the inestimable benefits of literacy upon your court.

Aethelberht: That's very kind of you but to be honest we don't have much call for literacy in the general way of things, being a warrior society and so forth. But insofar as we do – diplomatic correspondence with the Mercians, reminders to Charibert about the dowry and whatnot – I've got a roomful of scribes already doing it.

Augustine: Oh, you have...

Aethelberht: We're not complete barbarians round here. Well, yes, I suppose technically speaking we are, but Kent spent four hundred years in the Roman Empire so we've got a tradition of literacy. Not, I grant, a flourishing tradition but enough to be getting along with. Sorry old chap ... if there's nothing else...

Augustine: What about writing in Anglo-Saxon?

Aethelberht: Blimey, there's a thought. But I can't see the point. Even if we were writing to other Anglo-Saxons their scribes wouldn't be able to read it, would they? They only read Latin. And as for writing to the Franks or your man in Rome, even if they could read it, it would be gibberish seeing as they don't speak Anglo-Saxon.

Augustine: True ... mmm ... what about a law code in Anglo-Saxon?

Aethelberht: Ah now, that could be a runner. I can see the advantages in everybody knowing what crimes they mustn't commit. Preferably before they commit them. Go on then, tell me what it involves.

Augustine: Well, Anglo-Saxon isn't really compatible with the Latin alphabet so I might have to mess around some. Shouldn't be a problem but even so since no alphabet has more than a couple of dozen symbols I will have to re-invent and simplify your incredibly complex natural language into something more phonetic. You'll kind of recognise the new one but basically you'll have to learn it just like I had to learn Latin even though I'm a Tuscan-speaker. Which reminds me, I'll have to learn Anglo-Saxon in order to do any of this. No, wait, I can get a team of your scribes on the job since they already speak Anglo-Saxon and they will be able to understand my Latin instructions. Of course we will all have to learn philological techniques that haven't been employed since my own forefathers did it in central Italy a thousand years ago and unfortunately they didn't leave a blueprint. Never mind, we can learn on the job. Once we've finished we shall have to teach all your other scribes this new modified form of Anglo-Saxon in order for them to learn to write it but since they've already spent several years doing all this in the case of Latin they won't begrudge a few more years. After that it's all downhill.

Aethelberht: I suppose we might have to teach the crims how to read so they can read the law code but we'll cross that bridge when we come to it. How long will all this take? We're only a rude military caste when all's said and done. Even the scribes. Especially the scribes if you ask me. A ballpark figure will do.

Augustine: These massive cultural shifts always take longer than you think but what is it now ... 597 ... so we're probably looking at the late 590's ... early seventh century tops.

Or we can test out our third possibility, the one no academic historian would give house room to, the *Laws of Aethelberht* is bogus. To the unlearnèd layperson this may seem plausible

> **The only surviving early manuscript of the Laws of Aethelberht is in the Textus Roffensis, dating from the twelfth century, and it now resides in the Medway Studies Centre in Strood, Kent**

But unlearnèd laypersons are unlikely to be let loose on the problem because this would put in jeopardy one of the foundations of English, European and world history. The ranking academic authority can tell us the full immensity of what is involved

> **Wormald explains this more eloquently: "There is an at least indirect connection between the fact that England is today the world's oldest continuously functioning state and that English is its most widely spoken language. Its language and law are the most enduring marks of Englishness, its main claims to anyone else's attention. The history of both begins with Aethelbert"**

30

Unlike the *Gospels of St Augustine*, when it comes to the *Laws of Aethelberht* we are no longer in the business of confounding Popes and Archbishops of Canterbury. Not that we ever were – if you have swallowed the camel of the creator of the universe impregnating a Jewish woman with his only begotten son, you will have no trouble digesting an off-colour gospel book. They can be left to their own parochial concerns. For the rest of us, bereft as we are of divine guidance, the *Laws of Aethelberht* represents a 'paradigm anomaly'. We all love an anomaly. Life would be dull indeed were it not for those little bits that don't quite fit, the contradictions never entirely resolved, the coincidence too far. In the normal course of events they either get explained or they gradually fade from memory. But occasionally these hanging questions are sufficiently important they either have to be explained or our understanding of the world has to change – these are the *paradigm anomalies*. People will do more or less anything rather than change their world, so they first adopt the strategy of ignoring the problem and trusting it will fade from memory. However, it being such an *important* problem, this cannot happen and sterner measures are required. Pending its resolution, which surely will be forthcoming eventually, the anomaly has to be studiously and deliberately avoided by all available means. Taken together, these are what those in my line of work call 'careful ignoral' but which generally come under the blanket term of 'cognitive dissonance'.

'Careful ignoral' can last for centuries. Since Isaac Newton enters our story later on we might take, as an example of a particularly long-lasting paradigm anomaly, the orbit of Mercury. In the eighteenth century the educated world had settled down happily enough to a Newtonian Universe except the hyper-educated world of the university knew Mercury did not fit into it. Everything else in the universe behaved as Newton said it ought, save Mercury, whose orbit *wobbled*, just a little bit but sufficient to be unmistakably anomalous. Was the world to throw its newborn baby out because of one molecule in the bathwater? No, it was down to *observational error* so that was all right then.

By the end of the eighteenth century observational methods had improved a whole bunch but the anomaly remained. One or two savants offered up explanations but nothing flew. Newtonism survived, it was just too damned good. 'Observational error' survived along with it; it had to, one cannot have an impending sense of crisis looming over the entire universe. Physics can be its own worst enemy – it's one for all and all for one, no exceptions. By the nineteenth century observational methods had improved a whole bunch more and Mercury's anomalous orbit could be observed with greater and greater precision. Whatever the explanation, the least likely was observational error since that was the one area of astronomical endeavour that was truly motoring – unlike astronomy itself, which was stuck in suspended animation. Nobody noticed this. The more the observed universe grew, the more it stayed the same, the more Newtonian it became. Steady-state was good news! The universe was understood and did not require another Age of Giants to understand it all over again. [*Sotto voce*: "It's observational error or the abyss."] Finally Einstein examined the molecule rather than the bathwater, Relativity replaced Newtonian Physics, the baby was saved, astrophysics started growing by leaps and bounds.

The reason it took so long was 'careful ignoral'. Once it is recognised that observational error cannot hold because observational methods have improved so much, attention bears down on Mercury rather than the Universe, and the tail can be used to wag the dog. The anomaly, as we say, becomes the solution not the problem. The obvious question is 'What's unique about Mercury?' to which the equally obvious answer is 'It is the nearest body to the sun' which provides the even more obvious corollary 'The sun is perturbing the orbit of Mercury'. OK, it wasn't. The sun was perturbing the photons of light by which we were observing the orbit of Mercury so it was observational error all along, but that is why these things can take time. The point is you have to get past the 'careful ignoral' stage to get there.

In today's tightly woven world, whenever a paradigm anomaly is present, there ought to be a gaggle of academic subjects bearing down on it. Except they won't be, they will be *bearing away from it* because of 'careful ignoral'. Academic subjects are highly artificial constructs that have grown up higgledy-piggledy over the years. The boundaries between them always have some sort of rationale but it is ruefully acknowledged, even by academics, these demarcations are more often down to historical accident, bygone fashion and plain bricks-and-mortar inertia. This is true but not the whole truth. The boundaries can also be there because of *paradigm anomalies*. When everybody is moving away from a persistently unsolved problem via *careful ignoral*, the rent in the academic space-time continuum slowly becomes unbridgeable. What is more, the problem itself, existing in the netherworld between subjects, becomes essentially unexaminable because of the academic conventions that

1. one discipline does not interfere with the internal workings of another discipline
2. one discipline has to accept the specialist expertise of another discipline should it need to make use of its material.

If, say, molecular biologists have a particularly thorny problem to solve, they are not allowed to say, "Sod it, we're going to assume capillary action works *thisaway* – that should resolve the issue." Even if later it turns out it does. The upshot is that not only does the paradigm anomaly remain, it goes unremarked. Should anyone be so unwise as to draw attention to it, they will be greeted with either, "Not our problem, matey, try the department next door" or if it is too obviously an in-house problem, "Oh, no, not that old chestnut." Yes, that old chestnut, the one that will never grow into a tree, whose roots will never spread out under the building, never cause its curtain wall to fracture, never bring the whole gimcrack edifice crashing down, never provide conkers for the little boys and girls. It's all so terribly sad.

The *Laws of Aethelberht* is our Mercury. Should it ever get resolved, boundaries will change, empires will fall. But which ones? The first subject for toppling is Anglo-Saxon Studies. You may not have heard of this – it is mostly an American thing – but its raison d'être is that the Anglo-Saxon language is held to be Old English and English-speakers are so pre-eminent in academia, it is assumed Anglo-Saxon Studies is inherently a worthwhile and important area of academic enquiry. Were these assumptions not so entrenched, there would no more be Departments of Anglo-Saxon Studies than there would be Departments of Anglo-Roman Studies, of Anglo-Danish studies, of Anglo-Norman Studies. Without the language nexus the Anglo-Saxon period of English history would be less significant than the Tudors or the Stuarts and *they* don't get university departments of their own.

It is not to be wondered then that Anglo-Saxonists concentrate on that nexus, the Anglo-Saxon language, studying its variations over time and place, as recorded in the surviving documentation. So, an innocent might suppose, that means they pore over the *Laws of Aethelberht* with special vigilance, it being the earliest example of the said Anglo-Saxon language. No. The laws are *quite* interesting in themselves but, as the 'surviving documentation' is a twelfth century copy, doubtless expressed in the language of twelfth century copyists, it is not *very* interesting. Its language is sort of neither here nor there. Still it does form part of their remit so they are duty-bound to pass judgement on it. However, when it comes to the *authenticity* of the Laws of Aethelberht, the Anglo-Saxonists are faced with some real professional dilemmas which, all things considered, they would rather not face

1. They are trained to judge the language of documents written in Anglo-Saxon but the *Laws of Aethelberht* is agreed to be couched in twelfth century Anglo-Saxon so all that can usefully be said is there is nothing inherently un-sixth century about it.
2. They are trained to judge the content of documents and Anglo-Saxonists can point to a raft of other law codes to show there is nothing inherently un-sixth century about Aethelberht's laws.
3. They are not trained in judging the authenticity of physical documents, that is a matter for palaeographers, but palaeographers will be of no help because they will merely report yes, it is a twelfth century document.
4. If Anglo-Saxonists start questioning the authenticity of the *Laws of Aethelberht* and it turns out to be genuine, they will get a shed load of criticism not just for wasting their own time and money investigating something nobody thought worth investigating in the first place, they will be roundly condemned for giving credence to crackpots set on undermining the entire fabric of ... well, frankly who knows what their motives are. Are they French?
5. If it turns out to be bogus, the fact that the *Laws of Aethelberht* had hitherto been the earliest example of the Anglo-Saxon language, means the remit of Anglo-Saxon Studies has just got a whole lot smaller.

Best not to rely on Anglo-Saxon Studies. The historians will have to ride to the rescue. After all, for them, the Anglo-Saxon period is just another period in British History, no different in principle to the Tudors or the Stuarts. But no, there is a difference – the ground is already occupied. There are no departments of Tudor studies, no departments of Stuart studies, there *are* departments of Anglo-Saxon studies. For this reason alone few historians choose to specialise in the Anglo-Saxon period. But there are *some*. Are historians specialising in the Anglo-Saxon period in a position to challenge the *Laws of Aethelberht*? Of course they are, their daily lot is the examination of contemporaneous documents. Except in this case it is not a contemporaneous document but a twelfth century copy. No matter. An authentic copy is *nearly* as good as the real thing. But how near? How do you judge what is an *authentic* copy? You can't. It is an unfalsifiable proposition and we all know to leave those well alone.

Thank the lord for the linguists, they of all people will be professionally concerned with the earliest surviving example of the world's most important language, the *Laws of Aethelberht*. The more so as Anglo-Saxon is an Anglo-German language and the academic study of linguistics was founded by and is still dominated by English-speakers and German-speakers. One teeny problem. A swathe of academia is already studying the Anglo-Saxon language. They are called Departments of Anglo-Saxon Studies. With four thousand other languages just crying out to be studied, neophyte linguists would be ill-advised to specialise in one that has been, as it were, so thoroughly specialised in already. More to the point, were they native English- or German-speakers, they would risk being accused of subjective parochialism, even WASP syndrome. And nobody else is interested in Anglo-Saxon. If you do fancy a lifetime studying an ancient language which has a comfortably small literature yet still packs a historical punch, why not try Babylo-Assyrian or Old Church Slavonic?

And so, bringing up the rear, is that most powerful department on any campus, the English Faculty. There can be no doubt they will be focused on the veriest roots of English. Yes and no. Tenured members of the English faculty bear a scar. When they first turned up as first year Eng Lit undergraduates, they were forced to sit down and read Beowulf in the original Anglo-Saxon which is extremely hard work. What they thought they had signed up to was sitting around chatting about The

Floss on the Mill, which is not hard work. But that was in the bad old days. Universities now have to pay a lot more attention to the bums on the seats so for the most part the Anglo-Saxon component has been dropped from the English syllabus. Anglo-Saxon is still self-evidently important, being the veriest roots of English and all, but sitting around chatting about *Heaney's* Beowulf meets that requirement. However, some of the stuffier universities still insist on studying Anglo-Saxon in situ but it is unlikely the Laws of Aethelberht will get a mention. With the best will in the world, it's not *literature*, is it?

So the anomaly just stays there, minding its own business, while the academic subjects all around plough their merry way forth to pastures new. Actually pastures old because progress is unaccountably slow. So what? Progress is always slow, it's the diminishing marginal utility of epistemological enquiry, isn't it? No, it isn't. It's the fate meted out to academic subjects founded on faulty paradigms. So what would happen to those academic subjects were the anomaly eliminated and the paradigm corrected? That is unpredictable but it is always more than any of them can imagine. Not that any of them *can* imagine it because paradigm crashes are so rare few present practitioners would know what you were talking about unless they had read their Kuhn back in the day. The changes may be unpredictable, but the ripples will oscillate through the stagnant pool in increasingly violent ways.

At first all is calm. Were, for instance, the *Laws of Aethelberht* agreed to be bogus, it would be strictly a matter of housekeeping. Not routine – we're talking an entire conference to discuss the implications – but domestic. In-house not Augean stables. How would the argument go? Well, Aethelbert codifying laws and writing them up in Anglo-Saxon is nothing special, just early. Bede refers to it but that does not undermine Bede because, after all, the rejection of a twelfth century document does not mean Aethelbert did not in fact issue laws in Anglo-Saxon back in the sixth century. Moreover, the next speaker points out, the Anglo-Saxon Chronicle does *not* mention them even though it is rather keen on demotic law-codes, so that's one for the credibility of the *ASC*, isn't it? Which just about wraps things up. Next year in Marienbad, everyone?

Ah, but this might be a paradigm matter. Why so? Because Aethelberht's laws are the *first* and that makes a difference. You can't just slot them in and hoik them out willy-nilly – if they are no longer the first, something else must be the first. First law code? No sweat, the Anglo-Saxon Chronicle has a list of replacements for that role. First English writing? Could be more serious. Academic subjects do not ordinarily clean their dirty laundry in public but this time they may have to. The Guinness Book of Records will have to be amended for a start. At present the entry reads (don't look it up, I'm using a privately printed edition)

Oldest written English: **Laws of Aethelberht** c 600 AD

which in the next edition, with Aethelberht gone, will have to be quietly adjusted to

Oldest written English: **Cædmon's Hymn** 658 - 680 AD

Will anyone notice this first trickle in the dyke? Probably not. Excising Aethelberht's Laws from the canon does not affect the onward march of English history in any way. It does though throw the spotlight onto Caedmon's Hymn. On *Caedmon*. Is the understudy ready to go centre stage? Caedmon has always been a cherished but minor figure in England's pageant

> He was an Anglo-Saxon who cared for the animals
> at the double monastery of Streonæshalch (Whitby
> Abbey) during the abbacy (657–680) of St. Hilda (614–
> 680). He was originally ignorant of "the art of song"
> but learned to compose one night in the course of a
> dream, according to the 8th-century historian Bede. He
> later became a zealous monk and an accomplished and
> inspirational Christian poet

Some poetic license here clearly but how much exactly? What, for instance, is in a name? Nobody cared before but by an accident of manuscript survival Caedmon is now, as it were, 'father of English letters'. That is awkward on account of there being another 'Caedmon'

> Cadmus was credited by the ancient Greeks
> (Herodotus for one) with introducing the original
> Alphabet to the Greeks, who adapted it to form their
> Greek alphabet

A fascinating coincidence. What are the chances that Mr and Mrs Anglo-Saxon would name their son after a mythical Greek hero, the father of Greek letters, and that their little boy would grow up to be the father of English letters?

But it must be true because Bede, only a generation later and living just up the road, said so and he is famously scrupulous in his use of sources. Our very own Herodotus. No, what must have happened is Caedmon was born plain Albert or whatever and his patroness, the Abbess Hilda, renamed him in honour of the well-known Greek hero after his literary apotheosis. No, wait, that can't be right. Hilda, back in the seventh century, would have no idea her protégé would turn out to be the father of English letters – that's an accident of manuscript survival. Could it be Hilda, rather than Caedmon, that needed some 'rounding out'? Could it be Hilda rather than Caedmon that is required for the onward march of English history? When Classical Greek was more widely studied in Europe than it was in seventh century Northumbria? Maybe, maybe not. We will need to know a little more about this formidable patroness of the arts

> The prestige of Whitby is reflected in the fact that King Oswiu of Northumberland chose Hilda's monastery as the venue for the Synod of Whitby, the first synod of the Church in his kingdom. He invited churchmen from as far away as Wessex to attend the synod. Most of those present, including Hilda, accepted the King's decision to adopt the method of calculating Easter currently used in Rome, establishing Roman practice as the norm in Northumbria. The monks from Lindisfarne, who would not accept this, withdrew to Iona, and later to Ireland

Oh dear, we do have a tiger by the tail. This is the very *schwerpunkt* of our early history, the moment when 'Roman' Christianity triumphed over 'British' Christianity and set the course of 'English' history for the next nine hundred years until the sixteenth century when, by one of those twists in the whirligig of time, English Christianity replaced Roman Christianity after the Reformation. Dr de Hamel himself waxes lyrical about what effect this had on 'extant contemporaneous documentation'

> In 1568 Matthew Parker obtained licence from the
> Privy Council to take into his own custody any
> original manuscripts in England which would justify
> the Anglican Reformation in these terms and would
> provide tangible precedents for the Elizabethan
> agenda. Parker eventually commandeered about six
> hundred early manuscripts, mostly from the libraries
> of recently restructured medieval cathedrals or from
> former monasteries, including many of the oldest
> books then in England. He was the first truly great
> collector [*Meetings*, p. 13]

I don't think 'collector' exactly sums up what the Privy Council had in mind, but here's a thing. The present day successor of Matthew Parker – for the 'collection' is now in the Corpus Christi Library – is a gentleman called Christopher de Hamel. Back away from the desk, Chris. Put the tippex down, you know it's not worth it...

*   *   *

By this stage you may be wondering less about the *Gospels* of St Augustine and more about St Augustine. At the start of this journey we listed all the remarkable things about his book but they are nothing compared to the remarkableness of the man. Here is what historians believe to be his accomplishments between his reported arrival in England in 597 and his sadly early demise reportedly in 604. He was, according to historians, one of the

1. **greatest missionaries of all time**, instrumental in the conversion of England
2. **most significant church administrators of all time**, the first Archbishop of Canterbury, and thus the first executive head of the now worldwide Anglican community
3. **most effective land surveyors of all time**, laying out the boundaries between the sees of Canterbury and Rochester with such deftness they have survived from that day to this
4. **most notable linguists of all time**, the inspiration for transcribing into literary form today's most widely spoken language

5. **luckiest bibliophiles of all time**, owner of the book destined to become the oldest non-archaeological artefact in the country that developed the modern study of archaeology.

Before picking out your favourite Augustinian attribute, you might wish to address the more basic question: have we got the right Augustine? St Augustine (of Canterbury) is very famous to us Brits because we believe he founded Christianity in Britain but, to everybody else, St Augustine means St Augustine of Hippo, 354–430, who is by most people's reckoning the world's pre-eminent Christian philosopher. Getting two such famous figures confused seems implausible, yet academic historians would accept, if they gave it any mind at all, *our* St Augustine was almost certainly named for *their* St Augustine. Benedictine monks take a 'monastery name', normally of an apostle or a famous saint, as part of their vows, so presumably Benedictine Brother Augustine, as he must have been on his arrival in England, had chosen his monastery name in honour of St Augustine of Hippo. Which means, in a manner of speaking, both the *Gospels of St Augustine* and St Augustine's Abbey, Canterbury, are named for both saints. This gives rise to an intriguing possibility.

> Copy of minutes of a meeting at **St Augustine's, Canterbury**
> *Present*: My Lord Abbot
> Four apprentices

Abbot: You're all in imminent danger of being fired unless we can come up with some fresh income streams. I'm told you're our current hotshots, so pitch me ideas.
Apprentice One: It has to be pilgrimages. A bit passé, I know, but they're still getting bigger and there's no upside ceiling I can see.
Abbot: Don't you think we've already been down that road? We've practically beggared ourselves acquiring the latest must-see venerabilia. I know you novices think us higher-ups are on our knees all day praying but I can assure you we are mainly praying for ways to keep this whole operation afloat.
Apprentice Two: So what went wrong, pilgrimage-wise?
Abbot: Nobody came. Not in sufficient numbers. Who in their right mind is going to visit a place like Canterbury?

Apprentice Two: I don't follow you, your grace. We get swarms of visitors. We're on the busiest road in the country, halfway between London and Dover.

Abbot: One day out from Dover to be exact. Which is precisely why we were set up here in the first place, to service the cross-Channel trade. But they're travellers, not pilgrims.

Apprentice Three: What's the difference, they're all paying customers.

Abbot: You don't seem well-versed in the people business, son. Probationer-scribe are you? Let me spell out a few facts of life in the real world. A traveller arrives last thing at night, leaves first thing in the morning. What do you think our mark-up is on a single bed-and-breakfast?

Apprentice One: Four-in-a-bed!

Abbot: Even so. Now your pilgrim is quite a different animal. Assuming you've got your basic kit of in-house relics and shrines, which like I say we have more than enough of, plus your usual outstations within walking distance – in our case, the holy wells, a hermit's cave, couple of ...well you lot should know, you've all had to do your stints.

Apprentice Four: Yeah, when does that stop?

Abbot: When I say so. The point is, with pilgrims, we're talking seven days on average, according to last year's figures. And they spend. Offerings for a cure, charitable donations, passing the plate morning and evening, street collections for whatever it is that day. And before they leave, the souvenirs to show the folk back home, the specials you don't show the people back home. I promise you, to us one pilgrim is worth fifty travellers.

Apprentice Two: I still don't see the problem. We can service both, can't we?

Abbot: No, that *is* the problem. We can't. And it's a problem peculiar to us. Come on you lot, think about it. A pilgrim's got a choice of ... what is it now? ... two dozen places on the circuit. God knows how many independents. Where is he (increasingly *she* on the latest figures) going to choose for next year's trip?

Apprentice Four: Why not us? Like you said, we've got everything everyone else has.

Abbot: We've got one thing *more* than anyone else has. What's our

USP? Or, big clue, what's our *negative* USP? You've already identified it.

Apprentice Two: The cross-Channel travellers.

Abbot: Exactly. People don't want to come back from a pilgrimage to be met with "Oh, you went to Canterbury, did you? Passed through there a couple of times myself as a matter of fact. And on the way back too. Very popular place, Canterbury. Bit busy, for my taste. Everyone coming and going is not my idea of somewhere for a quiet contemplation of the eternal verities but there you are, it all depends what you're after, I suppose. Where you going for your next pilgrimage? London? Southampton? Nottingham Goose Fair? Only kidding. I'm green with envy."

Apprentice Two: With the greatest respect, your eminence, there's plenty of successful pilgrimage destinations in busy cities. Durham's top three. Norwich is on the up and up since they walled up that woman anchorite.

Apprentice Three: I heard about that. Couldn't we...

Abbot: We're not a fairground freak show. There's only two reasons you go to Durham: you either live there or you're going on pilgrimage there. If you do go on pilgrimage, people are impressed – you're impressed with yourself. Nobody badmouths Durham – or Norwich for that matter – they're nice and remote for most people, even a bit exotic. But Canterbury's forever doomed to be just the last stop-off before the Continent. There's no getting round that.

Apprentice Four: Unless we turn the situation on its head.

Abbot: Go on.

Apprentice Four: We might be the last stop for the Continent but that makes us the first stop for the Continentals.

Abbot: So?

Apprentice Four: Just because we're Transit City to the English doesn't mean to the Continentals we're not ... what were your words? ... *remote and exotic*. And as we happen to be the nearest pilgrimage centre to the Continent, they'll flock over in droves. Of course we'll have to do some decking out.

Apprentice Three: Decking out?

Apprentice Four: Put on attractions suited to the market. It can't be that difficult. Or expensive. For a start we can take that Blaise head out of storage. They love him over there.

Abbot: Yes, that's a very good idea. What's your name? Such a good idea my predecessor thought of it twenty years ago. But don't let that dishearten you, my boy, great minds think alike.

Apprentice Four: Clearly it wasn't such a good idea after all.

Abbot: No, it wasn't. Turns out pilgrims like things to be arduous but arduous in a certain kind of way. Apparently being seasick and getting drowned occasionally wasn't the kind of arduousness pilgrims like. That's why Blaise is back in the store cupboard. Come along, gentlemen, think! Your vocations depend on it.

Apprentice Three: One bloke didn't mind getting seasick.

Chorus: Huh?

Apprentice Three: Think it through. We're a Roman Catholic country, right? So it stands to reason someone must have brought it here from Rome.

Abbot: Some *one*? I hardly think mass social transformations are the result of one man ringing his bell. But it's Blue Sky Rules here so do, please, elaborate for the benefit of the rest of us.

Apprentice Three: Suppose it *was* one man ringing a bell – we don't know it wasn't – the point I'm trying to make is the bell-ringer must have come through Canterbury. Wouldn't that put us on the map, pilgrim-wise? First Christian in England and all that.

Abbot: And all what? Do you want us to put up a plaque in the town square saying "St Engleberht, Converter of the English, probably spent the night here on his way to London". What are the pilgrims meant to do, kiss the plaque? Re-enact his journey by spending the night here?

Apprentice Four: Blue Sky Rules, skipper.

Apprentice Three: Let's say London's unsuitable for some reason – we can fill in the details later – no, I've got it, after being seasick and half drowned St Engleberht found Canterbury a veritable paradise on earth. On land. So he settled here, built a church .... no, wait, let's make him a monk, he builds a monastery here...

Apprentice Two: Yeah, right. Once the monastery is up and running, and the conversion's in full swing, they'll need a chapel. Then a church, then a preceptory, then a ... we could be looking at a full-blown theme park. Pilgrims will surely flock to England's first monastery, first church, first everything.

Apprentice One: Especially as Engleberht died here and was buried here. The Tomb of the Christ Bringer. Heap big juju.

Abbot: Never mock the customer, son, she's your mother. Won't someone notice this place has been here fifty years, not five hundred?

Apprentice Three: Built on existing foundations.

Abbot: What's that supposed to mean?

Apprentice Three: Look at it this way. What is Engleberht actually going to put up in the circumstances? It can't have been anything very grand, wattle and daub or something. But, whatever it was, people liked the new religion, we know they did, so soon they have to pull that down and build something, probably timbered, on the site. Then it'll be a stone building, then ... well, eventually it'll be everything you see around us.

Apprentice One: In fact, fifty years is rather convenient. Who's to know any different? Some old codger muttering, "This was all green fields in my day"?

Apprentice Four: And it won't stop there. To glory England's First Christian, you have to glory the First Christian's vision of the future. We could be looking at a permanent Fighting Fund to repair the roof, build an extra wing, a transept, we could do with a new refectory. We're practically the new Jerusalem. Could even be some state funding in it.

Apprentice Two: Let's not forget *old* sells too. If we're now saying there are five hundred years of us being here, who knows what we'll be able to find with some creative digging. A Celtic cross, I expect, obviously pottery from Engleberht's period, a crypt that time forgot ... it's a gold mine.

Abbot: Yes, all very clever but unfortunately it will never work. We'd be named after him if he founded us. Or soon would be. Nobody's going to believe us if we suddenly change our name to St Engleberht's.

Apprentice Three: Unless he was called St Augustine...

Abbot: Really? Did he pop over from Africa on a long weekend break from writing the *Confessions*?

Apprentice Three: No, no. We all have to take a saint's name on completion of our novitiate and anybody sent from Rome to convert England isn't going to be a novice. So our man will have a saint's name. No reason why he wouldn't have taken the famous Augustine as his saint's name, is there? So, who's to say which Augustine we're named after?

Apprentice Four: The dirty great portrait of him in the sacristy for one thing.

Apprentice Three: Oh that. It's always struck me as just a stylised rendering of your typical early holy man.

Abbot: As it happens, you are correct. I was only a novice myself at the time but it was originally a Simon Stylites we got in part-payment for something, can't remember what, but old Gervase, young Gervase then, stuck on Saint Augustine's name. All right, no promises, but pilgrims aren't mugs, they'll want something tangible to show *this* Augustine really was here. What relics fit the bill?

Apprentice Four: With him being buried in the shrine we can't very well have his body parts cluttering up the place.

Apprentice Two: No, but we'll certainly have kept his old cope, won't we?

Apprentice One: And a shoe. People like a shoe, people identify with shoes.

Apprentice Four: And don't forget the simple bowl and spoon that was all he could carry with him o'er land and sea to far-flung Inglaterra. I get all weepy just thinking about it.

Apprentice Two: Plus a Bible. He must have brought a Bible with him, there wouldn't be one where he was going.

Abbot: We've got to watch the bottom line. Bibles don't come cheap. I think a gospel book is probably as much as he could manage, walking all that way.

Apprentice One: Unless he had a donkey. Everybody loves a donkey.

Abbot: No donkey.

Apprentice Four: Look, it's not relics we've got to worry about. We're going to need some big time interpolations seeing as how there won't be any mention of our Augustine in the sources.

Abbot: Yes, that has been tempering my enthusiasm too. Founding Christianity in England is going to get you noticed. And recorded. Who's been on the Documentation Course?

Chorus: We all have!

Abbot: That's more than I have. A word to the wise, all of you, the scriptorium is *not* the path to preferment.

Apprentice Four: Attendance is mandatory now.

Abbot: Good God, what a sign of the times. You'd better put me in the picture.

45

Apprentice Three: The basic situation is that nothing much has survived from the Anglo-Saxon period – no surprise there, there wasn't much to start with – but what's amazing is even so we've got a continuous history of England from when the Romans left right up until today ... and it's all thanks to the chance survival of a few scholarly works that are, I've forgotten the word...

Apprentice Four: *Extant.*

Apprentice Two: Not quite extant. We only have modern copies of the three that matter though, to be fair, they do cover the period completely and in uncanny detail.

Abbot: Yes, the Holy Trinity – Gildas, Bede and the Anglo-Saxon Chronicle. Even I know that.

Apprentice One: If we box clever, we won't have to worry about Gildas.

Abbot: Oh? I'd have thought he'd be central if we're talking early Christianity in England.

Apprentice One: No. This St Augustine of ours creates a paradigm shift. Gildas is native *British* Christianity, in other words a hangover from the Roman Empire version – Constantine the Great, Nicaea and all that – with a bit of Celtic and local interpretation mixed in. A right mess, frankly. Had a hard time keeping outright paganism at bay – not that you could tell 'em apart most of the time. Anyway, what we were taught – and I presume what you were taught, gaffer – was that over time this got replaced by our own *Papal* Christianity. The point is, now we can have Augustine arriving *after* Gildas, which means no mention of him *by* Gildas, so there's no need to change anything *in* Gildas.

Apprentice Four: It makes for a fabulous story as well. Gildas is your John the Baptist figure, old school tub-thumper, lacerating everyone with his jeremiads, country going to the dogs, et cetera et cetera. Along comes Augustine, your Jesus figure, to introduce Christianity proper with set rules and a hierarchy and an orderly civilised life is enjoyed by all. Rejoicing all round, brave new world, it's the Age of Augustine ... it's the Age of Canterbury!

Abbot: All right, don't get carried away. What are we going to do about Bede? If we're going to put Augustine after Gildas – when's that...?

Apprentice Two: Died five-seven-o, plus or minus.

46

Abbot: Then we're going to run straight into Bede. You're not going to tell me we can avoid Bede too.

Apprentice Three: No chance of that but then Bede's a problem for everyone so it's accepted procedure *adjusting* Bede. *Redacting* as it's known in the trade.

Abbot: Yes, I know all about that – good grief, I'm an abbot – but it's one thing adding *but Griswald later had a second son by another Anglo-Saxon princess who...* and then relying on page spaces, copying errors, who's got the original and what not, but this is a different order of magnitude. It's certainly going to involve at least a whole section de novo plus references back.

Apprentice Four: Gets worse, I'm afraid. This would be so fundamental, and as far as Bede is concerned, so early, all Bedes will have to read the same. I mean, word for word the same. There are a dozen libraries out there and they've all got their Bedes, they'll all need to be squared. It's a major undertaking, guvnor, it's going to cost you, no getting around it.

Apprentice One: On the other hand, by the same token, it's going to be a one-time operation. Once all the exemplars are Augustinianised, future copies will take care of themselves. Nobody's going to tamper with it if it's fundamental. So, if it's a one-off, can't we just lob some dosh to make it stick?

Abbot: *Lob some dosh*, the man says. If you've all been on the course you'll have done your networking. You don't have to tell me about the Scribal Freemasonry of the Novitiate, I have to deal with the complaints about the pornography you're always sending one another. In any case you could be knocking on open doors. A major revision in this league creates plenty of opportunities for other people too. Work out the likely winners and losers, start calling in favours and I might be able to find something in the kitty for the holdouts. Now what about the Anglo-Saxon Chronicle?

Apprentice Two: Above our pay grade, boss.

Abbot: Yes, all right, you'd better leave that with me. Entre nous, there's already a list as long as your arm of proposed amendments at the national level. Today's Bretwalda is tomorrow's unperson. I should think a Complete Recall must be on the cards fairly soon. I might be able to hurry things along a bit. I still count for something at the

Abbots' Conference. Anyone not playing ball won't get any help from us when they want some local nobody getting martyred by Danes just because they need a new saint.

Apprentice Four: You scratch my balls and I'll...

Abbot: Yes, thank you. Now, if that's all, we had better...

Apprentice One: We haven't done Rome yet.

Abbot: Rome? What Rome? Why do we need Rome pushing their nose into our trough?

Apprentice One: Sorry, cap'n, it's unavoidable.

Abbot: Why so?

Apprentice One: If our Augustine was sent from Rome to convert us, there's bound to be something or other in the Vatican archives about it. Adding England to the portfolio would be quite a bag.

Abbot: Anything's do-able in Rome for a price. A fat price. Which we haven't got. No pull either, to speak of.

Apprentice Two: *All roads lead to Rome.*

Abbot: What's that supposed to mean?

Apprentice Two: All English roads that lead to Rome go via Dover. There's only one Dover Road and it happens to come past our door. So all the pence in Peter's Pence go past our door. Seeing as how we are officially tasked with responsibility for this stretch, everything owing to Rome from anywhere in England could be subject to, shall we say, a certain amount of *flexibility* about how long it takes to get past our door.

Abbot: We wouldn't dare ... would we?

Apprentice Two: Just sayin'.

Abbot: Well don't.

Apprentice One: No harm in finding out what's involved at the Roman end, though, is there?

Abbot: Well, I suppose not. It might broaden your education.

Apprentice Three: First off, it means picking the right pontiff. If we're talking post-Gildas, 570 plus or minus, plus a bit of mayhem to account for the disappearance of contemporaneous documentation at this end, we're looking at Augustine arriving around 600. That's good for us, it means Gregory the Great.

Abbot: Bad for us, surely? I'd feel a lot more comfortable tinkering with the historical record of somebody a bit less famous.

Apprentice Three: With respect, chief, you haven't been on the course. Obscure popes are bad news. Let's take a 'for instance'. You come up with a Papal Bull saying something like "I award Anglorum Rex permanent dominion over Scotland, signed Urban the Umpteenth", you have a word with your man in the Curia and it goes straight into Vatican Registry, copy to London, copy to York. Job done, or so you think. A few years down the line some contrarian soul – I imagine probably a contrarian Scotch soul – is going to want to know what else good old Urban the Umpteenth put his name to in the course of his all too obscure reign. There won't be much, not in the Registry, not in the Archives. There's a very good chance with a lot of these old popes there won't be anything at all *except* your precious Bull. The Scotch will cry 'foul' and who's going to argue with them? The English of course but nobody else will want to get involved one way or the other. It might take, it might not take. Complete lap of the gods.

Abbot: But with Gregory the Great...?

Apprentice Three: Chalk and cheese. There's reams of his stuff. They've probably got a wing named after him. A lot of it genuine for all I know. And it's *important* stuff, important to the Church, important to everyone. That's why he's called 'the Great'. You go round raising red flags about Gregory material and you'll have half Christendom on your case. So yes, it's expensive getting it in, but once it's in, it's in for keeps.

Abbot: Let's go back to my idea about Peter's Pence. All kinds of security implications where cash is concerned ... what with pirate scares in the Channel and so forth. They can go on for months ... years ... better safe than sorry ... it's our Christian duty to look after it ... it'll be earning interest, so nobody loses...

Chapter 3

The Book of Kells

The *Book of Kells*, on display at Trinity College, Dublin, is seen by half a million people in an average year, while poor old Augustine over in Cambridge has to make do with one properly vetted academic every other month. Why the difference? It is largely a question of how much a country has to put in the shop window. The British have more than they can handle whereas the Irish have to scratch around a bit. Whether this is a good thing or a bad thing depends, I suppose, on whether one wants to be a nation of shopkeepers.

By now we are thoroughly familiar with the methodology for exposing ancient manuscripts as forgeries but this time we have an additional arrow in our quiver. Guilt by association. If the *Gospels of St Augustine* is bogus and the *Book of Kells* turns out to be a horse of a similar colour, we are home and dry. Here are the Top Ten Characteristics the two books have in common

1. Both are illustrated gospel books
2. Both are purportedly from the depths of the Dark Ages, Augustine *c* 600 AD, Kells *c* 800
3. Both were created with blank pages in various places
4. Both contain 'marginalia' written on the blank pages
5. Both sets of marginalia consist mainly of land charters
6. Both sets of land charters are in favour of the monastery that owned the book
7. Both sets of charters are written in a mixture of Latin and the local language
8. Both books are missing their opening pages
9. Both books have anachronistic illustrations
10. Both books lack any historical evidence for the first centuries of their claimed existence.

Guilty as charged. Next! What's that you say? Guilt by association is not probative in the court of Irish opinion? You demand proof? Are you sure, these things can be traumatic. Oh, I see, you feel that having emerged from the chronic torpor of de Valera's pietism to become a Celtic Tiger you're now ready to cast off the shackles of faux Irish history and become a Celtic Lion? Possibly. Let's see how you get on with the *Book of Kells* first. Dr de Hamel, not an Irishman as far as I know, is Old School

> This 'most precious object of the Western world' is now
> a national monument of Ireland at the very highest
> level. It is probably the most famous and perhaps the
> most emotively charged medieval book of any kind. It
> is the iconic symbol of Irish culture [*Meetings*, p. 99]

'Medieval' in the academic lexicon encompasses what the rest of us call the Dark Ages. Dr de Hamel wants to be helpful but, as a scholar, must speak truth to power

> It is, however, historically likely that the Book of Kells,
> the most Irish of all works of art, was actually made in
> what is now Scotland... [*Meetings*, p.139]

But he is swift to reassure

> ...and, after all, *Finnegans Wake* was written in Paris,
> and its Irishness is not in doubt either [*Meetings*, p.139]

Well no, not really, Chris. *Finnegans Wake* was written by an Irishman who happened to be living in France when he wrote it. The *Book of Kells*, according to you, was written by scribes of undisclosed nationality in a Scottish monastery which happened to have been built by Irishmen two hundred years earlier

> Recent research has revealed that Irish labourers built
> 102, boulevard Haussmann, where *À la Recherche
> du Temps Perdu* was written. Dublin authorities have
> demanded the return of Proust's original manuscript.
> The Bibliothèque nationale is considering the request.
> No early decision is anticipated.

Dr de Hamel should maybe heed his own advice

> Politics and sense of national identity are so embodied
> in the Book of Kells that even the most experienced
> of medievalists have learned to tread very cautiously
> [*Meetings*, p.138]

51

Not me. I'll be wading straight in with me boots.

*   *   *

We can, however, all agree provenance must come first

> The date and place of origin of the Book of Kells have
> attracted a great deal of scholarly controversy. The
> majority academic opinion now tends to attribute it to
> the scriptorium of Iona, a monastery founded around
> 561 by St Columba in western Scotland. Following
> a Viking raid in 806 the monks took refuge in a new
> monastery at Kells, County Meath. It must have been
> close to the year 800 that the Book of Kells was written

Don't like that 'must have been'. Still, let's go with the flow. Presumably
such a prestigious book at such a prestigious monastery will attract its
fair share of mentions in the historical record. But no! It disappears
into the Irish gloaming then emerges for a brief sighting two hundred
years later

> The earliest historical reference to the book, and
> indeed to the book's presence at Kells, can be found in
> an AD 1007 entry in the Annals of Ulster

That *is* vexing. But paradoxically it is also good news because while 1007
may seem a bit late for a supposedly c. 800 document, it unequivocally
disposes of the canard that the *Book of Kells* might be an English
forgery. The English, in the form of Strongbow's Anglo-Norman
expedition, only arrived in Ireland in 1169, which is a great relief. For
the book, I mean, not necessarily for the Irish. Even so, this critical item
of provenance holds good only if the *Annals of Ulster* hold good. Given
the importance, we had better undertake a quick check

> The Annals of Ulster (Irish: *Annála Uladh*) are annals
> of medieval Ireland. The entries span the years from
> AD 431 to AD 1540. The entries up to AD 1489
> were compiled in the late 15th century by the scribe
> Ruaidhrí Ó Luinín, under his patron Cathal Óg Mac
> Maghnusa, on the island of Belle Isle on Lough Erne in
> the province of Ulster. Later entries (up to AD 1540)
> were added by others

That *is* vexing. The *Annals of Ulster* date from the 'late fifteenth century' and while maths has never been my strong suit I'm confident 'late fifteenth century' comes after 1169. The canard has landed.

Irish historians are not in the least bit fazed. The extant physical manuscript of the Annals of Ulster may date from the 1490's but it is *copied from earlier material*, that is the nature of annals. Ireland is no different from any of the other countries of Europe in lacking physical *contemporaneous* documentation for early history and has to rely on annals based on earlier material. As a matter of fact, and not a lot people know this, Ireland is peculiarly blessed with annals

Name of Country	No. of Annals*
Ireland	33
Wales	5
England	16
Scotland	5
Normandy	5
France	17
Germany	21
Spain	8
Italy	12
Belgium	1
Lithuania	10
Denmark	16
Switzerland	5
Hungary	5
Poland	7

* Don't write in, the numbers are only indicative

But there is a reason for this: the Irish need annals more than most. All the other European countries feature from time to time in one another's historical sources so they can, after a fashion, be cross-checked. But not Ireland. For some unfathomable reason nobody ever has anything to say about Ireland. This is all the more noteworthy because Irish *missionaries* pop up quite a lot and do quite important things, yet nobody ever says, "What ho, Kilian, thanks for christianising Thuringia and eastern Franconia, we really needed it. But now you're here, could you tell us a bit about this Ireland of yours ... for our records. It must be some place, sending out little old you all this way to convert little old us." [For *your* records: Saint Kilian, born *c* 640, Mullagh, County Cavan, 'Apostle to the Franconians', beheaded by Duke Gozbert of Würzburg, AD 689. Though not, as we shall see, for my records]

The Irish did not need cross-checking, they had their gospel books, and they surely are contemporaneous documentation, attested to as such by everybody qualified to give an opinion. Of course gospel books are not historical sources (except possibly for the Life of Jesus) but the land charters written in their blank spaces are. And here's another thing you probably didn't know – the individuals named in the gospel book charters cross-check with the individuals named in the annals! The one confirms the other, whichever way round you care to put it. What is more, we are in a perfect position to judge the whole construct since not only are the *Annals of Ulster* generally considered to be the most important of all the Irish annals, the most important entry in that annal is the one for the year 1007 because it confirms the existence and whereabouts of the *Book of Kells*. So, the single most pored-over passage in Irish historiography is the 1007 entry in the *Annals of Ulster*, the very one we ourselves are most interested in. We had better do some poring-over of our own just in case they missed something

> **A.D. 1007: The great Gospel of Columkille, the chief relic of the Western World, was wickedly stolen during the night from the western sacristy of the great stone church at Cenannas on account of its wrought shrine**
> [N.B. *Gospel of Columkille* = Book of Kells, *great stone church at Cenannas* = Kells monastery]

It would appear they did miss a couple of things. The bit that told them it is a forgery and the bit that told them when the forgery was done. Did *you* spot them? If you did, you have the makings of a first class forgery-detective. If you got one, you should consider a career in the Garda CID. If you didn't spot either, you probably already have a career as an Irish historian.

The entry was purportedly written in 1007, so it follows the 1007 annalist felt able to judge the *Book of Kells* was the 'chief relic of the Western World'. Even allowing for local pride this is an unexpected nugget of information for him to possess since according to Dr de Hamel

> **Then the lights go out on stage. Vikings, plague, famine, and the struggle for survival preoccupied the country. Almost no important manuscripts survive from Ireland later than the Book of Kells. When the rest of Europe began to wake up to the arts of manuscript illumination, Ireland had disappeared from sight** [*Meetings*, p.126]

So one must wonder how the annalist was able to come to his judgement. Who was his source for the Book of Kells being the 'Chief Relic of the Western World'? Reading de Hamel correctly, turn-of-the-eleventh century Ireland was not on the European map. Viking pillagers apart, nobody much went *from* Ireland, nobody much went *to* Ireland. But at least one intrepid soul must have done both – the annalist's source. Apparently he did the rounds of the European cultural hotspots, inspected everybody's top of the range artefacts, canvassed opinion about what the cognoscenti reckoned ought to be in the running for Europe's chief relic, concluded the *Book of Kells* was there or thereabouts, went back to Ireland, had a word with one of their top annalists and the annalist filed away the exceptionally cheery news that Ireland's very own contender, the Book of Kells, was one of the, if not *the*, chief relics of his day and noted the fact when he came to write up his annal. You might think I am being fanciful but this must have occurred at some time because, by a supreme irony, the Book of Kells truly is The Chief Icon Of The Western World! Even I know that. It is just that no eleventh century Irish annalist could have known that. Mistake Number One, the smoking gun, the one that betokens forgery.

Mistake Number Two is more subtle, more damning, more precisely diagnostic of when the forgery took place. The person responsible for the information in the 1007 entry, if he lived in and around 1007, was not just a fearless traveller, not just a faithful rapporteur, not just a fine connoisseur, he was a geographer of unparalleled acuity. How do we know? Because this all-seeing, all-travelling, all-knowing colossus *also* knew there was something called 'the western world'. Those of you who think the concept is less St Columba and more Christopher Columbus have been misinformed. The eleventh century Irish already knew it. And we know why they knew it. They had their very own Christopher Columbus – St Brendan the Navigator, *c* 484–*c* 577, the bloke who discovered America for the Irish. Everyone knows that!

> **There are over 100 manuscripts of the story across Europe, as well as many additional translations**

*   *   *

Can we at least agree on the background? The early Dark Age in England, say 400 to 600 AD, was very dark indeed, leavened only by the penumbra of whatever civilised values had been bequeathed by the Roman Empire, 0 to 400. The early Dark Age in Ireland was much the same except for the Roman Empire bit, the Romans never got that far. Dr de Hamel confronts the puzzle with his customary fair-mindedness

> **... the Book of Kells is so famous that it is easy to overlook that Trinity College in Dublin owns no fewer than five other early Irish Gospel Books which are even older. They may have less decoration but they are nevertheless stupendously precious relics of insular civilization, and, in truth, these half-dozen manuscripts together make up almost the entire corpus of such survivals from early-medieval Ireland** [*Meetings*, p.123]

Dr de Hamel is saying the *Book of Kells*, together with similar but earlier productions, comprise the sole evidence of Ireland having any 'civilised values' at this time. This burst of literary creativity cannot have come via the Roman Empire, so the challenge is to identify where it did come from. Dr de Hamel is kind enough to tell us

> **At one level, these Gospel Books describe nothing, for they are not local chronicles but standard Latin translations of religious texts from far away. At the same time, this is itself extraordinarily revealing about Ireland. No one knows how literacy and Christianity had first reached the islands of Ireland, possibly**

56

Well, a civilisation which could produce nothing but gospel books, so
a lot hangs on them. Actually, a bit more than 'a lot' because the four
centuries associated with the gospel books, roughly 400–800, is the one
and only time, according to academic historians, that Ireland made a
significant contribution to the wider world. And what a contribution
it was!

Fifth century	St Patrick converts Ireland to Christianity
Sixth century	St Columba sets out with his fellow-Irish missionary monks to found the monastery at Iona
Seventh	Ionan missionaries convert Scotland to Christianity and re-Christianise much of England
Eighth/ninth	Scottish and English missionaries of the 'Ionan movement' establish monastic scriptoria throughout Western Europe
Tenth/ eleventh	these monastic scriptoria are a vital component in the rise of Medieval Europe
12th to 20th	Western Europe is mainly responsible for everything we have around us in the world today

Well done, the Irish. Only one Western European country got left
behind in this magnificent and inexorable rise from local rags to world
riches. You will remember which one

From zero to hero to zero. Still, we know the hero part is true because
1) we have the *Book of Kells* along with its five prototypes and 2) we
have Columba's monastery on Iona. Hold up! We might have to scrub
the Iona part because despite this tiny island being per square foot

among the most examined parcels of land anywhere on earth, no archaeological evidence of any kind of Dark Age monastery has ever been found. The Vikings were infamous for their systematic pillaging but making off with the archaeology is a new low even for them.

*   *   *

We must not be downcast. As with the Gospels of St Augustine, the *Book of Kells* contains a number of marginalia which, whatever the shortcomings of other lines of enquiry, at least provide a firm *terminus ante quem*. As usual these marginalia consist of land charters drawn up in favour of the Potala Temple in Lhasa, Tibet. Only kidding, it was Kells monastery in Ireland! No, really.

> **The family of Kells have granted for the support of pilgrims, Ardcanna, i.e. Baile Ui Uidhrin, with its mill, and with all its land, and Baile Ui Chomhgain, with all its land, and with its mill, to God, and to Columbkille, and to the Bishop o'Cellaigh, the senior of all the men of Meath, and to Maelmuire O'Robhartaigh, head of the Disert, on the third isle of the Ides of November, the feast of Martin, in the year when the kine and swine of Ireland perished by a pestilence**

So the *terminus ante quem* of the Book of Kells is confirmed to be the year when the kine and swine perished.

*   *   *

One of the institutional problems of Irish history is that Ireland is not a major player in world history so receives scant attention from the international fraternity of historians. On top of which, some of the documentation is in Irish, a language unfamiliar to the international fraternity of historians. As a result Irish history tends to be exclusively the preserve of historians who happen to be Irish. It goes without saying they are trained to the highest academic standards but it does mean peer review, bestowals of tenure, establishment of paradigms –all the basic necessities of academic subjects – tend to be *Irish*. Furthermore, as with all academic subjects, some things particularly interest the specialists, some don't. In the case of Irish history, ancient land charters fall into the second category

> How early the ancient Irish began to commit their contracts and covenants to writing has not yet been determined, nor indeed made the subject of enquiry by anyone qualified to arrive at just conclusions

An English historian's judgement, to be sure, so for an Irish view of the charters in the *Book of Kells* we must perforce turn to the non-academic but authoritative official guide

> The charters are of a date some centuries later than that of the Book of Kells itself, in which they are found ... it will be necessary to distinguish between the date of the charters, i.e. of the contracts to which they relate, and of the copies now extant in the Book of Kells ... which were probably transcribed from the original deeds into this sacred and venerable book in order to secure their preservation

For those who do not speak guide book officialese, this is telling us there are three distinct time periods

1. when the Book of Kells was written
2. when the charters were written
3. when the charters were copied into the Book of Kells

This is the same peculiar sequence followed by the land charters in the Gospels of St Augustine but *they* relate to a different set of time periods. To compare them, we shall need the specific dates for the Book of Kells. One we have already

1. when the Book of Kells was written was c. 800

So when were the charters written into it? Over to the guidebook

> Along the lower margins of the last of these pages and all over the once-blank leaves which follow them are transcripts of various contracts written in the medieval Irish language. There are more elsewhere in the manuscript too. They all relate to land around the monastery of Kells between the late eleventh century and 1161

which gives us

2. when the charters were written was between, say, 1080 and 1161

and to finish off

> The period at which they were transcribed into this book may be conjectured from the character of the writing and the contractions, which would appear to belong to the latter part of the twelfth century ... the hand-writing of these documents, as they are now found in the Book of Kells, is not coeval with the persons whose names are mentioned in them

so that gives us

3. when the charters were copied into the Book of Kells was around 1175

and since we have already established a similar official timeline for the *Gospels of St Augustine* we can draw them together

600 Gospels of St Augustine created
800 Book of Kells created
950 English monks have the idea of copying their land charters into the Gospels of St Augustine
1175 Irish monks have the idea of copying their land charters into the Book of Kells

This must be a case of great minds thinking alike because there is no known connection between tenth century Anglo-Saxon monks in Kent and twelfth century Irish monks in County Meath. Or was it a case of lesser minds thinking alike? That is the implication of the timeline in the unauthoritative *M J Harper Guide to Anglo-Irish Illustrated Gospel Books*

1200 Monks create Gospels of St Augustine
1200 Monks create Book of Kells
1200 Monks put spurious land charters in Gospels of St Augustine
1200 Monks put spurious land charters in Book of Kells

This brings us to the charters themselves which doubtless will provide rich pickings for both our guidebooks. Here is a particularly juicy one from the official version as mediated by Dr de Hamel

> Those here record deals such as that Ua Breslén, priest
> of Kells, and his kinsmen have bought for 18 ounces of
> silver a piece of land known as Muine Choscáin, with
> its meadow and turbary (the right to cut turf, or peat),
> extending to the west as far as the mire of Donaghmore,
> as witnessed by very many people (try to imagine them
> all gathered noisily around the manuscript), including
> Oengus, grandson of Rancán, full chief of Sil Tuathail;
> Ferdomnach Ua Clucáin (d.1114), successor of Colum
> Cille, with all the community of Colum Cille; Ua
> Dúnán (d.1117), senior cleric of the north of Ireland
> and of Domnall son of Flann Ua Maelsechnaill, king of
> Tara (1087-94); and Ossin, son of Echtgal, doorkeeper
> of Kells [*Meetings*, p.112]

Wow! All those people gathered noisily around to witness a property transaction. Sounds more like a pub than a solicitor's office. I expect they're one and the same in rural Ireland. Dr de Hamel is not just impressed by this turnout of local and national worthies, he may be over-impressed

> The names sound magical and redolent of a very
> ancient world... [*Meetings*, p.113]

If I were a scholar, even a scholar writing for a general audience, I would steer clear of phrases like 'sound magical' and 'redolent of', certainly when they are bracketed with 'absolutely'

> ...they also localise absolutely where the book must
> have been at that time... [*Meetings*, p.113]

But 'absolutely' is absolutely required because

> ...[T]hese inscriptions are actually the only early
> evidence that this manuscript is indeed the great
> Gospel which belonged in the eleventh century to Kells
> [*Meetings*, p.113]

But why were the charters written into the *Book of Kells* in the first place? The guide book has already told us they were

> ... transcribed from the original deeds into this sacred and venerable book in order to secure their preservation

A modern insurance company might have something to say if you tried 'securing the preservation' of your favourite cufflinks by placing them in a Fabergé egg and how right those insurance johnnies would have been because, according to Dr de Hamel, thieves made a bee-line for the venerable book rather than the original deeds

> as described in the account of its theft from the church there in 1007 [*Meetings*, p. 113]

This incident explains how the *Book of Kells*, as per the Gospels of St Augustine and as per Forgery 101, comes to have its opening telltale pages missing. Dr de Hamel explains in some detail what has been 'lost'

> The manuscript is no longer complete ... it probably lacks up to about a dozen leaves at the beginning [ ] The text opens [with] the last column of a lost list ... of Hebrew proper names which occur in the Gospels of Matthew and Luke, in alphabetical order (it may surprise you to find alphabetization already in use in the eighth century) [*Meetings*, pp. 128,106]

Nothing surprises me anymore about the *Book of Kells* but, unlike the English 'wear and tear' explanation for Augustine's missing pages, the Irish have a much more exciting tale to tell. It is set out in that most renowned of crime reports, the 1007 entry in the *Annals of Ulster*

> the great Gospel of Columkille, the chief relic of the Western World, was wickedly stolen during the night from the western sacristy of the great stone church at Cenannas [Kells] on account of its wrought shrine

but now there is some good news

> The manuscript was recovered a few months later— minus its golden and bejewelled cover—"under a sod". The force of ripping the manuscript free from its cover may account for the folios missing from the beginning and end of the Book of Kells

However, Dr de Hamel has an advantage over both Irish annalists and Irish historians – he spent thirty years working for Sotheby's, where he gained invaluable insights into the *modus operandi* of art criminals

> **The robbers were interested only in the value of the precious metal, and they may have been Vikings. There survive elsewhere records of other manuscripts stolen around this time, including a Psalter in a jewelled binding looted in 1012 from the abbey of Saint-Hubert in Luxembourg, and the Stockholm Codex Aureus, stolen by Vikings from Canterbury in south-east England and immediately ransomed back again, doubtless without its binding** [*Meetings*, p.99]

So many books, so many missing front pages. But how about those crazy Irish Vikings! They get their mitts on one of the chief treasures of the Western World, worth a fortune on the ransom market, and promptly ruin the re-sale value by ripping out pages just for some scraps of precious metal. But then they do something even crazier

> **The thieves of the Book of Kells presumably stripped it and discarded or buried the worthless text** [*Meetings*, p.99]

Well, which is it? They are two very different things. Fleeing thieves having stripped off the jewels might 'discard worthless text' but taking time out along the way to bury it is bizarre. Dr de Hamel is just toying with us, he knows very well what they did. They chose the bizarre option

> **This Gospel was recovered after two months and twenty nights, its gold having been taken off it and with a sod over it** [*Meetings*, p.98]

This presents a conundrum. Ireland in the early eleventh century was composed of billions of turf sods (estimates vary), and after 'two months and twenty nights' the trail had clearly gone cold. But they found it! All in a day's work for the Irish manuscript hound.

*   *   *

Talking of Sotheby's, we really must have a look at the illuminations, always a prominent feature of illuminated gospel books. The *Gospels of St Augustine* had that very distinctive framing of the Last Supper which led Dr de Hamel to propose – he didn't have much choice – the strikingly similar portrayal in the Bayeux Tapestry had to be derived from it. What he omitted to mention was this very particular framing, the front-on shot of Jesus at the centre of a large table flanked by apostles on either side, is not only

a) one of the most enduring images in European art, but
b) made its debut in the Gospels of St Augustine

Yes, that's right, the *Gospels of St Augustine* was first in the field for one of the biggies of European Art History. The *Book of Kells* is going to have to go some to match its English rival. It certainly makes a gallant effort

a) *the* most enduring image in European art is the Madonna and Child
b) there is a Madonna and Child in the Book of Kells

Then the Irish leave the rest of the field standing. Dr de Hamel is right on the ball this time

Apparently it is the earliest representation of Virgin and Child in European art [*Meetings*, p.113]

*   *   *

Enough knockabout. You know the drill by now. We have a bit of a laugh at other people's expense then we get down to the hard graft of systematic historiographical revisionism. Kells needed ancient land charters for precisely the reason Canterbury did. The Angevins had arrived. Along with their law courts. So we shall need another potted history of land tenure (Ireland). Don't worry, this will also be mercifully short. Mercilessly short, the Irish might say.

Year Dot– Nothing known except, as detailed above, land charters
1169 AD in gospel books

1169 Anglo-Normans, hereinafter "the English", arrive

1169 to now The English occupy certain areas, notably and famously The Pale of Settlement around Dublin where they construct a thoroughgoing feudal system and shire administration. All land is individually owned with or without formal title. The rest of Ireland, literally Beyond the Pale, is left under native control in which land is owned via an inchoate mix of common clan ownership, the local magnate's holdings and individual owner-occupation. Title to any particular piece of land is founded on customary rights mediated by force and, reportedly, the occasional written land charter in gospel books. Over time, and under a variety of pressures, the whole of Ireland shifts more and more to the English way of doing things.

Where does Kells fit into this? Snugly. Kells (the place) sits right on the cusp between the Pale and native Ireland. Kells (the monastery) was presumably positioned there *because* it was on the cusp. The Normans, under various names, had a characteristic method of empire-building which was to physically occupy and administer areas where it was worth it and to use indirect methods where it was not worth it. The Norman way of doing things can be observed in France, England, Wales, Scotland, Calabria, Sicily, Greece and Palestine, and is a policy followed by most successful imperialists. Specifically in Ireland, this meant the Pale was physically occupied and administered while the rest of Ireland was subject to a hearts and minds policy and control at a distance via intermittently compliant native rulers. The hearts-and-minds was essentially Christianity. This was new to Ireland – pray cleanse your mind of such will o' the wisps as St Patrick and St Columba – and was not so much a religious thing as a civilisation thing. Literacy for one thing but much, much more.

Ireland in the twelfth century was literally pre-historic. It had the basics: agriculture at the subsistence level, industry at the craft level, trade at the barter level, but if the Irish wanted to join civilised Europe – and like all pre-historic societies they sort of did and they sort of didn't – then it was the monasteries' job to make sure they mostly did. But if you want to read further about this, consult more fully documented episodes like, say, how the Cistercians operated in the north of England or the Augustinians in Scotland. It is all routine. We are only concerned with Kells and its problems over land title.

Kells monastery faced both ways. It had to satisfy the demands of legal challenges from the Pale as well as native Irish resistance to its land grabs. So when a land charter is transcribed onto a blank page in the Book of Kells

> The king of Tara has granted, that is, Maelsechnaill,
> son of Conchobhar O'Maelsechnaill, and the comharba
> *successor* of Columbkille, that is, Domhnall Mac
> Robhartaigh, with all the ecclesiastics of Kells, in like
> manner, both priest, and bishop, and professor etc etc

it is not so important whether there were real kings of Tara or whether Columbkille, i.e. St Columba, had a successor, but it is important both sides should be satisfied there was some kind of legitimacy to the current ownership. It was not just a land grab. To acquire this aura of sanctity and legality there was no need necessarily to go to all the bother of physically building a monastery. The *Book of Kells* was more than sufficient on its own

> Later in the twelfth century, the monastery was
> dissolved with the abbey becoming a parish church and
> the Book of Kells continued to be kept there. Catholic
> landowners acquired the land

This last phrase is a slip of the pen. The writer is so used to *Pale = Protestant* and *Irish hinterland = Catholic* he has quite forgotten it was the Pale that was Catholic in the twelfth century, the Protesting Party was in the hinterland. But either way when

> In 1152, the Synod of Kells completed the transition
> of the Colmcille's [St Columba] establishment from a
> monastic church to a diocesan church. A later synod
> reduced the status of Kells to that of a parish

it has to be borne in mind, whether there were synods held at Kells or anywhere else, there was *no monastery there* before the twelfth century. We know this from the archaeology. There is none. What in fact was going on was

Following the Norman invasion of Ireland, Hugh de Lacy was granted the Lordship of Meath in 1182. The religious establishments at Kells continued to flourish under their Anglo-Norman overlords. Kells became a border town garrison of the Pale and was the scene of many battles, between Bréifne Irish and Hiberno-Normans, both of whom had heavily intermarried

Both of whom had heavily intermarried. When you read "Catholic landowners acquired the land" you should be crucially aware that, in Ireland, religion is always super-important but not nearly as important as land ownership.

∗   ∗   ∗

The land charters in the *Gospels of St Augustine* were in a mixture of Latin and Anglo-Saxon and now we find those in the *Book of Kells* are in a mixture of Latin and Irish. In both books we have the expected language and the unexpected language, the literary language and the local language. The Anglo-Saxon writing came as something of a bolt from the blue because it was the first new literary language in Europe for a thousand years and was achieved in the most inhospitable of environments. The Irish, it turns out, were just as enterprising

The earliest identifiable writer in the Irish language is Dallán Forgaill, who wrote the *Amra Coluim Chille*, a poetic elegy to Colum Cille [St Columba], shortly after the subject's death in 597. The *Amra* is written in archaic Old Irish and is not perfectly understood

Not perfectly understood but it must be true because

It is preserved in heavily annotated versions in manuscripts from the 12th century on

Lightning has not only struck twice it seems to have struck at the same hour. England's claimant for first dibs was the *Laws of Aethelberht*, which was also dated to "shortly after 597", Augustine's arrival at Canterbury. This could present difficulties since, as we know, if *x* and *y* are conjoined and *x* is discredited, then *y* goes too. But this is not a hang together or hang separately situation because historians are adamant *x* and *y* have no connectivity. They came from quite different places: England from Rome and Ireland from ... where was it? ... oh yes, north Africa. It is a simple case of independent co-invention and the British Isles specialises in these.

Anyway, not quite co-invented because Dallán Forgaill's Columban elegy is only the earliest example of Irish by an *identifiable writer*. What about all those anonymous scribes writing marginalia into the gospel books Dr de Hamel told us about?

> ... Trinity College in Dublin owns no fewer than five other early Irish Gospel Books which are even older and ... make up almost the entire corpus of such survivals from early-medieval Ireland [*Meetings*, p.123]

Give an Irishman a gospel book and he will write an Irish land charter in it

> Old Irish, dating from the 6th century, used the Latin alphabet and is attested primarily in marginalia to Latin manuscripts

It is fascinating to hear that sixth century Ireland was a land of estate agents requiring land charters and presumably law courts to superintend the whole business though we know the Irish have a yen for this sort of thing because they did it all over again in the twelfth century when the Anglo/Irish Norman/Angevins set up shop. But first time round, not only did the Irish do it before anyone else, not only did they do it in even more unpromising circumstances than anyone else, they had a much harder job on their hands putting Irish into a Latin alphabet than anyone else.

Anglo-Saxon and Latin are members of the same Indo-European (Western Branch) language family so the one can be more or less shoehorned into the other's alphabet. The Irish language by contrast is stuck out in a more distant linguistic clade alongside Welsh, Scots Gaelic, Breton, Cornish, Manx, Cumbric and Galician. Whether any of them are even Indo-European is dubious but I cannot pronounce on the matter because linguistics is a resolutely unscientific endeavour consisting mainly of people sitting around wondering whether this word sounds like that word and if it is decided they do, splitting the difference and coming up with a notional word that gave birth to them both. If you do this for enough words you can produce whole ancestral ur-languages to which you can give stern-sounding names. Soon you will have enough proto-languages to make proto-phylae and eventually a complete proto Linguistic Tree of Life. "Not so much of the 'proto' if you don't mind, the fruit of the tree is real enough – the languages we speak today – so the tree can't be far off the mark, can it?"

It would all be harmless enough, crossword puzzles for the advanced wordsmith, were it not for the fact that what we live in today are nation states and nation states tend to be based on language. Who gets to live in what nation state is a very Big Question indeed. Linguistics being more than ordinarily subjective means it is more than ordinarily subject to national interests.

When the academic study of languages got going in the eighteenth century one of the Bigger Questions of the day was how English-speakers were to govern a country containing lots of people speaking Welsh, Irish and Scots Gaelic. 'By the usual means' was the answer to the question but the usual means now included language studies. Not though with the outcome we might anticipate in our own more enlightened times. The speakers of Celtic (or Goidelic or Gaelic or Brythonic or Proto-Celtic or P-Celtic or Q-Celtic) languages were anxious to be enfolded into the high status Indo-European family for their own reasons (frankly, to do with low self-esteem) and the empire-building English were just as keen to enfold them. Whether everyone really was one linguistic happy family has remained something more a matter for political consumption than for internal debate amongst linguists. Academics generally are obliged to be politically correct because they are, directly or indirectly, paid from the public purse and those who pay the piper are entitled to hear their favourite songs off the first album.

Ireland's first album was *The Celtic Revival*, when St Columba emerged from his Irish fastness to found Iona whence his disciples spread the length and breadth of Western Europe bearing their message that the key to the future was monastic scriptoria. Which to some extent they were, though they had nothing to do with Ireland. But I agreed at the outset I would not dwell on the fact that Ireland has no history at all before the Anglo-Normans arrived and what they do have is bogus. Even if I tried, my credibility would be shot to hell on account of myself being Anglo-Norman (mum from the Îles Normandes, dad from the Elephant & Castle).

Chapter 4

Cuthbert's Gospel

England's equivalent of the Book of Kells is the *Lindisfarne Gospels*. The English are just as reverent towards their own magnificently illuminated manuscript though perhaps with a more English reserve. I'm saying now't on the subject. It's one thing upsetting the Irish, I have to live with the English. But the people who brought you the *Lindisfarne Gospels* came up with several less celebrated gospel books so I'll talk about them instead. This is Dr de Hamel on one of the Durham School's other productions

> **[the] lovely early eighth century 'Saint Cuthbert Gospel',
> now in the British Library ... apparently interred at an
> early date with the body of Saint Cuthbert, who had
> been enshrined at Lindisfarne in 698** [*Meetings*, p.81]

Steady on, Christopher, the British Library has just shelled out nine million acquiring it for the nation *because* it was interred with the body of St Cuthbert. This is not the language the nation wants to hear. How would the Dutch like it if you said *The Night Watch* was apparently painted by Rembrandt? How would Europe like losing its oldest book

> **The St Cuthbert Gospel retains its original binding and
> is the oldest intact European book**

How would the world like to lose the Laws of Physics because, if the *Cuthbert Gospel* was interred with Cuthbert, they will have to go too. So a bit less of the 'apparently' if it's all the same to you, *Doctor* de Hamel, it's make-your-mind-up time for the universe as we know it. I don't mind upsetting the universe.

✳   ✳   ✳

But we begin, as ever, with the provenance

> The book takes its name from Saint Cuthbert of
> Lindisfarne, in whose tomb it was placed, probably a
> few years after his death in 687. Although it was long
> regarded as Cuthbert's personal copy of the Gospel, to
> which there are early references, and so a relic of the
> saint, the book is now thought to date from shortly
> after Cuthbert's death ... intended to be placed in St
> Cuthbert's coffin

Strictly speaking, grave goods are not permitted in Christianity. It has always been a mark of the faith one must arrive in the next world unencumbered. Dispensation for saints would be uncanonical in any age. However this is not the main issue here. The *Gospels of St Augustine* raised that tiny doubt about whether the book was personally owned by the great man, or was only 'closely associated' with the great man, and here is the exact same awkwardness with *Cuthbert's Gospel*.

It is another case of the infamous 'either-or' technique. Pilgrim-trade promoters have a compelling reason for things to be personally owned by the titular saint because they are dealing with *relics*, objects of devotion, the devotee has to touch that which the saint has touched. History-trade promoters are obliged to be more circumspect; they have to follow the sources and with *Cuthbert's Gospel* there is a problem with the sources. The chief authority for all things Cuthbertian is Bede and Bede does not mention the book in the coffin. This is perplexing because it was the 698 AD discovery of the uncorrupted body in its coffin that persuaded Bede to write Cuthbert's biography and generally launch the Cuthbert Cult. It is hard to credit so vigilant a historian as Bede, living just a few miles away, omitting mention of a gospel book clutched in his hero's hands. The mugwumps at the British Library think they can get away with the old 'apparently' dodge

> It was created in the late 7th century in the north-
> east of England and placed in St Cuthbert's coffin,
> apparently in 698. It was discovered when the coffin
> was opened in Durham Cathedral in 1104 on the
> occasion of the removal of Cuthbert's body to a new
> shrine

They are essentially arguing the *Cuthbert Gospel* was slipped into his coffin in 698, eleven years after his death, as a sort of thank-you present from his grateful Lindisfarne followers, a post-mortem carriage clock if you will. No reason to tell Bede. Yeah right! Everybody else gives this version short shrift

It was probably a gift from Monkwearmouth-Jarrow Abbey, where it was written

A good start but, by being specific about where the book was written, the standard version runs into this problem

Bede (672-735) was an English monk at the monastery of Saint Peter and its companion monastery, Saint Paul's, now Monkwearmouth-Jarrow Abbey

so Bede is firmly back in the picture because he was actually there when the gospel book was being prepared. But now he can be sidelined by the old 'either-or'

It was probably a gift from Monkwearmouth-Jarrow Abbey, where it was written intended to be placed in St Cuthbert's coffin when his remains were placed behind the altar at Lindisfarne in 698, or in the next few decades

'In the next few decades' would put it after 735 when Bede is safely dead. There is no problem with the book itself – that could come from any decade. In fact, looking at it today, it could come from Amazon but, unlike the Gospels of St Augustine or the Book of Kells, *Cuthbert's Gospel* has an astonishingly complete early provenance. Too complete, it turns out. You just can't win in the ancient manuscript game. If you too want to play The Compleat Journeyings of Cuthbert's Gospel, you will need a map and a pencil. Draw lines linking Lindisfarne, Jarrow and Wearmouth, then one over to the Lake District, then, without taking your pencil off the paper, back to Easington, then on to Chester-le-Street, down to Ripon, back to Chester-le-Street, but before you get there pause at Durham, then a dotted line down to Belgium, back up to Clitheroe, Lancs, and finally down to London and the British Library. Do not worry if some of these places are unfamiliar. We are going to have another potted guide.

Lindisfarne is one of the best-documented places in all Dark Age Europe. Nothing remarkable about that, it is hallowed ground, the Holy Island. Not so well-evidenced *under*ground as no ecclesiastical archaeology before the twelfth century has ever been found anywhere on Lindisfarne. But it is a tiny island and archaeological digs have been practically an annual event for as long as anyone can remember so it won't be long now. Or could there be a reason for this dearth of archaeology? Those of us who form the metropolitan elite have scarcely heard of St Cuthbert but he is the much loved patron saint of the north-east. They have even named a duck after him, the cuddy duck. This is what the rest of us call the 'eider duck' because of our fondness for eiderdowns so it is entirely feasible Dark Age Geordie monks were such hard cases they not only eschewed fancy bed coverings, they didn't bother with bedrooms. Or walls and roofs. That's it! They were hedge priests, prototype Wesleyans, living rough, preaching in the open air, not requiring buildings of any kind. Obviously they would need a tarpaulin when working on the *Lindisfarne Gospels* but that would not leave archaeological traces either. It all fits.

Wearmouth and Jarrow are habitually conjoined in historical accounts

> **Monkwearmouth–Jarrow was a twin-foundation English monastery, located on the River Wear, at Monkwearmouth, and the River Tyne, at Jarrow. Its formal name is The Abbey Church of Saint Peter and Saint Paul, Monkwearmouth–Jarrow**

Historically conjoined they may be but geographically they are separated, Wearmouth and Jarrow being seven miles apart, so a Wearmouth-Jarrow Abbey might seem a bit of a stretch. "Coming to the refectory, brother Ambrose?" "Just getting me Nikes on." It was different in Bede's day

> **At the age of seven, Bede was sent to the monastery of Monkwearmouth by his family to be educated by Benedict Biscop and later by Ceolfrith. Monkwearmouth's sister monastery at Jarrow was founded by Ceolfrith in 682, and Bede probably transferred to Jarrow with Ceolfrith that year**

I know what you're thinking. Can we trust the sources? No need for doubt on this occasion

> **The dedication stone for the church has survived to the present day; it is dated 23 April 685**

which is a tremendous relief because the archaeologists have been falling down on the job *yet again* and no archaeological evidence has been found at either place earlier than the twelfth century. It was probably thanks to these idle drones we didn't get the gig

> **The twin Anglo-Saxon monastery was the UK nomination for World Heritage Site status in 2011**

But to be fair to them perhaps there was not much archaeology to be found

> **The golden age of Monkwearmouth-Jarrow began to draw to a close in the late 8th century, as Northumbrian monasteries became vulnerable to Viking raids, with Monkwearmouth-Jarrow itself being attacked in 794 (the second target in England of the Vikings, after raids on Lindisfarne in 793). They were destroyed by the Danes about 860, and seem to have been finally abandoned in the late 9th century**

Technically the second and third targets in England of the Vikings since it is unlikely alien intruders would know they counted as one. But anyway, here ended the brief but glorious history of Jarrow, Wearmouth, Monkwearmouth and/or Jarrow-Monkwearmouth. Except for an afterglow so extraordinary, they're making a film about it. Places everybody, we're going for a take. Camera One, on Herald, prepare for half shot, turn to camera, Herald. Nice and loud, cue Herald, *"Thusly the renowned twin foundation, pride of the northern lands, perished as if it ne'er had been. Two hundred years then passed in dolorous silence".* Good, hold that shot, we'll put in the dissolve post-production. Camera Two, medium shot on Norman knights, keep those horses steady ... pan back to clergy ... that's nice, clergy, begin your walk through ... no, strut! you're lords of creation, remember ... someone talc that tonsure ... that's good ... and cut away ... Camera Three, close up talking head ... where's the talking head, someone get the talking head ... okay, look straight at the camera, nice and natural, authoritative but not patronising ... and cue talking head

> **The *Libellus de Exordio* traces the continuity of Durham's history, and in particular William of Saint-Calais's expulsion of Durham's clerical community in**

> 1083 in order to replace it with a group of Benedictine
> monks drawn from Wearmouth and Jarrow

A nice bit of heritage history. Somebody has decided to re-use two long-abandoned sites, seven miles apart, in order to build two brand new monasteries and staff them with two brand new sets of monks. Get UNESCO back on the line

> William de St-Calais was a medieval Norman monk,
> abbot of Le Mans, who was nominated by King
> William I of England as Bishop of Durham in 1080.
> During his term as bishop, St-Calais replaced the
> canons of his cathedral chapter with monks, and began
> the construction of Durham Cathedral

The plotline though will never do for a docu-drama. We've got cathedrals being built when there is already a cathedral chapter there, we have whack-a-mole monasteries, we have gospel books hopping in and out of coffins, we have historians and archaeologists chasing their own tails. We will need a script doctor for this one which I suppose means muggins. I would certainly start by getting rid of this William de St-Calais character. Never heard of him

> In addition to his ecclesiastical duties, he served as a
> commissioner for the *Domesday Book*. He was also
> a councillor and advisor to both King William I and
> his son, King William II, known as William Rufus.
> Following William Rufus' accession to the throne in
> 1087, St-Calais is considered by scholars to have been
> the new king's chief advisor

Oh, *that* William de St-Calais. Second most important man in the country. Obviously I've heard of *him*, I just hadn't connected him with Durham. Bit of a feather in Durham's cap I should say. But back to the story-line. In Norman power politics, there are snakes as well as ladders

> However, when the king's uncle, Odo of Bayeux, raised
> a rebellion against the king in 1088, St-Calais was
> implicated in the revolt. William Rufus laid siege to St-
> Calais in the bishop's stronghold of Durham, and later
> put him on trial for treason. A contemporary record of
> this trial, the *De Iniusta Vexacione Willelmi Episcopi*

Primi, is the earliest surviving detailed contemporary report of an English state-trial

Another one for the Guinness Book of Records. What was the outcome?

Imprisoned briefly, St-Calais was allowed to go into exile after his castle at Durham was surrendered to the king. He went to Normandy, where he became a leading advisor to Robert Curthose, Duke of Normandy, the elder brother of William Rufus. By 1091, St-Calais had returned to England and regained royal favour

It all sounds disturbingly familiar but here is the part that interests us

During his bishopric, St-Calais stocked the cathedral library with books, especially **canon law texts**

Not just canon law texts

The *Libellus de exordio*, a historical work of marked literary character composed and compiled in the early 12th-century, relates the history of bishopric and church of Durham and its predecessors at **Lindisfarne and Chester-le-Street (*Cunecacestre*)**

All very well but what connects Durham, Lindisfarne and points in between?

What historical continuity the *Libellus* finds comes from the constant presence of the community's patron, **Saint Cuthbert**. The miracles worked in Cuthbert's name during the late Anglo-Saxon period were particularly flamboyant, and the *Libellus* contains engaging accounts of some of these, including the miracle of the three waves (when Cuthbert turned a portion of the Irish Sea into blood in order to prevent his followers from taking his relics out of England, see *Libellus* ii.11), the foundation of Durham (when Cuthbert's body, being moved across England on a cart, refused to be moved, signalling his desire to remain at Durham, see *Libellus* iii.1), and several picturesque deaths visited upon the enemies of Cuthbert's devotees

Good enough for me but carping non-believers might demand some 'forensics'. Everyone's a CSI expert. Would a body satisfy you?

> According to the *Libellus's* preface, the work was carried
> out on the orders of the monastic leadership of Durham
> Priory; probably it was Prior **Turgot** himself who
> commissioned it. The latest datable contemporary event
> mentioned in the core of the text (albeit obliquely) is
> the opening of the tomb of **St Cuthbert** for his removal
> into the new **cathedral of Durham, 29 August 1104**

and that body is still in Durham Cathedral, so there. Alongside Bede as a matter of fact so it was a good thing somebody jotted down all the stuff about Lindisfarne, Jarrow and Monkwearmouth or we could easily have gone wrong. On a technical note, Bede is a 'Venerable', not a full-blown saint, so there is no point in asking for a DNA test on his remains – they are long gone – but Cuthbert is not just a saint, he is a top saint, with an uncorrupted body, so if you are a Catholic pathologist there could be prospects there. Before you start demanding an exhumation order though – and good luck facing down the wrath of the cuddyduckers – bear in mind that when they opened the coffin in 1104 the body was clutching *Cuthbert's Gospel* so it could scarcely be anybody else. It would probably be more useful getting an exhumation order for brain cells at the British Library.

∗   ∗   ∗

We turn with relief to the actual book – its detailed provenance and relationship to the Laws of Entropy. At present it is in good shape...

> Its finely decorated leather binding is the earliest
> known Western bookbinding to survive, and both the
> 94 vellum folios and the binding are in outstanding
> condition for a book of this age

...considering its trials and tribulations. We know how it started life because it was

> intended to be placed in St Cuthbert's coffin when his
> remains were placed behind the altar at Lindisfarne in
> 698, or in the next few decades

St Cuthbert died, according to Bede, in 687 and was buried on Lindisfarne. Being only fifty-three and having led an active outdoor life as a hermit, he was probably in pretty good shape. Lindisfarne may be cold and damp but it is sandy and well-drained so eleven years in Lindisfarne soil will not have done Cuthbert's body appreciable harm. In 698 he is moved inside, out of the elements, and although we have no information about the building (that's the one they can't find) we can reasonably assume the body will be in goodish condition in 698, or 'a few decades later', when *Cuthbert's Gospel* joins Cuthbert inside the coffin. There is no talk of reliquaries so it was presumably placed reverently in Cuthbert's all but intact hands. Or by his side. Underneath his head. Let's not get into details because we have, at this point in proceedings, a fairly full description of the package as a whole:

1 x coffin	wood, temporarily stone, wood
1 x body	reasonable condition
94 x folios	calfskin, brand new, top quality
1 x binding	cowhide, brand new, top quality

For the next hundred and seventy-five years the 'package' remains in this moderately preservative condition. A coffin inside a rudimentary structure facing out to the North Sea would not be best practice today but it could have been a lot worse. Then it got a lot worse

> **In 793 Lindisfarne was devastated by the first serious Viking raid in England, but Cuthbert's shrine seems to have escaped damage**

They may have looked inside the coffin but *Cuthbert's Gospel* has no fancy jewelling on the cover so it was evidently in no danger from the smash-and-grab brigade. However, according to reports, more serious threats were looming

> **In 875 the Danish leader Halfdene (Halfdan Ragnarsson), who shared with his brother Ivar the Boneless the leadership of the Great Heathen Army that had conquered much of the south of England, moved north to spend the winter there, as a prelude to settlement and further conquest. Eardulf, the Bishop of Lindisfarne, decided the monastery must be abandoned, and orderly preparations were made for the whole community, including lay people and children, to evacuate**

Not forgetting 'the package', their most prized possession. It was not designed for carrying so some modifications were in order and, thanks to our sources, we know what they were

> It was possibly at this point that a shelf or inner cover
> was inserted some way under the lid of Cuthbert's
> coffin, supported on three wooden bars across the
> width, and probably with two iron rings fixed to it for
> lifting it off

No update though about the condition of the now two hundred year old Cuthbert but liquefying cadavers may be a good medium for preserving calfskin and cowhide. We just haven't done the tests. But with the Danes peering over the horizon, whither coffin, body, book?

> They set off inland and spent the first months at an
> unknown location in west **Cumberland**, near the River
> Derwent, probably in the modern Lake District.
> Eardulf tried to hire a ship on the west coast to take
> them to Ireland

No luck. Nothing for it but to return to more familiar surroundings

> Then they left the more remote west side of the country
> and returned to the east, finding a resting-place at
> Craike near Easington, County Durham...

But they had to be foxy about it

> ...close to the coast, well south of Lindisfarne, but also
> sufficiently far north of the new Viking kingdom being
> established at York

and how nicely they had judged the political situation

> Over the next century the Vikings of York and the
> north became gradually Christianized, and Cuthbert's
> shrine became a focus of devotion among them also

This is good to hear but let us hope the devotion did not extend to opening the coffin too often because that could only accelerate the chemistry pertaining to body liquids, calfskin and cowhide. But at this point the organic brew catches a break, stability is at hand

> The community established close relations with
> Guthred (d. 895), Halfdene's successor as king, and

received land from him at Chester-le-Street. In 883 they moved the few miles there, where they stayed over a century, building St Cuthbert's Church, where Cuthbert's shrine was placed

Never put *stability* and *Vikings* in the same sentence

In 995 a new Danish invasion led the community to flee some fifty miles south to Ripon, again taking the coffin with them. After three or four months it was felt safe to return, and the party had nearly reached Chester-le-Street when...

Go on, have a guess

1. The Danes caught up and slaughtered the lot of them
2. Christianised Danes fought a pitched battle with the pagan Danes and Cuthbert was saved
3. They stopped for a breather and then resumed their journey to Chester-le-Street
4. They stopped for a breather and built Durham Cathedral

...their wagon became definitively stuck close to Durham, then a place with cultivated fields, but hardly a settlement, perhaps just an isolated farm. It was thought that Cuthbert was expressing a wish to settle where he was, and the community obeyed. A new stone church—the so-called White Church—was built, the predecessor of the present Durham Cathedral

He's coming home, he's coming home, Cuthbert's coming home. Not literally, Durham seems to have been one of the few places in the north of England Cuthbert did not visit, dead or alive, but suffice it to say 'Cuthbert had found his home'. Or I suppose technically 'Cuthbert had founded his home'. Anyway, coffin/body/gospel book had finally reached their last resting place and for a century or more reposed undisturbed until in 1104 some curious soul lifted up the lid, felt around a bit and plucked out the gospel book. Not a nice job to ask of anyone but straightforward enough because, although the body was five hundred years old and possibly a bit squidgy round the edges, *Cuthbert's Gospel* was, to use the classic phrase of the book trade as well as the British Library

in outstanding condition

Worth nine million pounds of anybody's money. Your money, taxpayers' money. Not my money, I'm a writer, I don't pay tax. O Lord, bring forth that day.

Chapter 5

The Durham Factory

Those who study the past have an ingrained fondness for things 'from the east'. This is not because of unconscious sun-worship on the part of practitioners in theology, history, archaeology, anthropology et al but because all these disciplines were founded by, and are still dominated by, people clustered at one end of the world's largest landmass. The *western* end. (Including its western extension in the next landmass). In their pioneering days, academic disciplines needed to frame hypotheses about how things got going but the theoreticians were faced with a problem. At that stage of human knowledge, it was not known how things did get going but there was a need for making assumptions to get the *academic disciplines going*. In such circumstances it is best to frame hypotheses that propose it all happened 'long ago' and 'far away'. Inevitably, if the world is being looked at from a western perspective, this means 'to the east' (occasionally, as with Out of Africa, 'to the south').

So far, so good. Then bad. Academics are very good at filling in details of pre-existing theories but very bad at challenging pre-existing theories, so these from-the-east hypotheses rapidly got *filled in* with a wealth of compelling detail. It quickly appeared to all concerned that these 'founding hypotheses' were exceptionally well supported. They were certainly well filled in. "The evidence is overwhelming," as they often put it. Since academic subjects are transmitted generation to generation by people who have passed their exams lecturing people who want to pass their exams, these founding hypotheses tended not to change generation to generation. As academia is held to be the highest intellectual authority in the world, nobody else was much disposed to take issue. But this is all strictly ivory tower; the world makes different arrangements for the important stuff.

The academic discipline of History is based on the study of contemporary documents so history has to begin with the invention of contemporary documents a.k.a. *writing*. This is held to have taken place 'in the east' – specifically along the Fertile Crescent of the Middle East – as were other notable advances in human activity such as agriculture, metallurgy and organised religion. East to west, there to here, them to us. That is the general picture. But at some stage it had to stop. With all the intellectual heavyweights clustered at the *western* end, there must have come a point when the tide turned and everything started going west to east, here to there, us to them. It follows *when* this happened is one of the most momentous events in the whole history of the world. Worth getting right. And illustrated gospel books are at the heart of the matter. In fact, *forged* illustrated gospel books are at the heart of the matter. They triggered the change! You won't believe this, you ought not to believe it, but you might believe it when we get to the last chapter.

Meanwhile, we shall need an outline history of gospel books. The Gospels themselves are held to be of the usual Eastern/Fertile Crescent origin and, though this is not as cut and dried as they would have us believe, we shall apply the hornet's nest principle and move swiftly on to the earliest gospel *book*. It is not a long journey because, history being history, i.e. the study of surviving contemporary documents, the earliest record of the Gospels will be somewhat closely aligned to the earliest surviving gospel book. This is widely considered to be the *Codex Sinopensis* which, true to form, is of Eastern/Fertile Crescent origin

> **It was written in the 6th-century. The style of illustrations suggests Syria or Palestine (even Mesopotamia) as the place of its origin**

However, the dating technique is not what most people would call 'rigorous'

> **the Sinope Gospels (*Codex Sinopensis*) has been dated, on the basis of the style of the miniatures, to the mid 6th-century**

nor is its provenance what most people would call 'full'

> **The codex was purchased in 1899 at Sinope, in Turkey (hence its name), by a French officer from an old Greek woman. Its text was published by Henri Omont in 1901**

But anyway, now the illustrated gospel book had been launched, it followed its destined path east to west and by the end of the sixth century we arrive at our own old favourite, the *Gospels of St Augustine*

> The main text is written in an Italian uncial hand
> which is widely accepted as dating to the 6th century
> – Rome or Monte Cassino have been suggested as the
> place of creation

and which, as we have been so reliably informed, reached England *c* 600 AD. Turkey (or Syria or Palestine or even Mesopotamia) to Canterbury in a few decades is impressive but is this the cue for the great flood-reversal to begin? Is this finally when once 'we' get our hands on something, it is 'watch out world'? Move over Sumer, move over Babylon, move over Alexandria, move over Athens, move over Rome, move over Byzantium, the Irish and the Northumbrians are coming. Certainly, on the narrow illustrated gospel book front, the official view is that it was.

> the Echternach Gospels, created around the year 690
> in Lindisfarne, was taken to Echternach Abbey in
> Luxembourg. The scriptorium at Echternach would
> then become the most influential centre for Hiberno-
> Saxon-style manuscript production in central Europe

But is officialdom jumping the gun? If both Lindisfarne and Echternach are pumping out Hiberno-Saxon-style manuscripts at roughly the same time, there must be a sound argument that it is still east to west, them to us, Luxembourg sending coals to Newcastle. Given this just might be the most significant event in the history of the world, it is worth nailing down. The orthodox view is adamant: it must be Lindisfarne to Echternach because the *Echternach Gospels* is only one of many similar productions attributed to turn of the eighth century Northumbria. No less than five of their gospel books have come down to us. Cue another potted history, 'history'

1. *The Lindisfarne Gospels*
   Created *c* 700 AD at Lindisfarne and used there as a gospel book. Carefully hidden during Viking raids except they found it once and took away the front cover. Coverless but unbowed, the book was taken to Chester-le-Street when Lindisfarne was abandoned in

875. Sometime around 950 an Anglo-Saxon gloss was added, the scribe writing the translation word for word above each line of the existing Latin text, thus creating the first Gospels in English. First and last for a goodish while because, give or take, it was to be five hundred years until Wycliffe, Tyndale and King James once more resumed the task of translating the Gospels from Latin into English. Not that translating was the most difficult part of the exercise facing the Anglo-Saxon scribe, that would be the ticklish business of writing tiny letters on parchment that had been in daily use for two hundred and fifty years. You can test just how ticklish for yourself if you've got plenty of two hundred and fifty year-old parchment to practise on. You can use a felt tip pen because Anglo-Saxon scribes working on the *Lindisfarne Gospels* weren't above the odd cheat with modern aids themselves

> **Eadfrith seems to have used a leadpoint more than three hundred years before the medium was generally adopted in Western Europe ... when executing the final versions, he must have placed a strong light source behind the parchment ... in a manner akin to a modern light-box. This would indeed be a stunning invention, not until Cennino Cennini in the fifteenth century was a similar technique described in writing**

Funnily enough, the *Lindisfarne Gospels* disappears for roughly the same period as English Gospel translations, only emerging into the light of day in Elizabethan times. It passes through various hands until 1753 when it is given to the British Library where it remains to this day, in tiptop condition, pride of the Library, pride of the nation.

2. *Cuthbert's Gospel*
Created around 700 in Lindisfarne or Jarrow or Wearmouth or Jarrow-Monkwearmouth. Placed in St Cuthbert's coffin on Lindisfarne around 700 or soon after, it re-emerged in the twelfth century as a relic in Durham Cathedral, where visitors were allowed to wear it round their necks in a leather bag. Possibly one of them walked off with it because this book too was lost to history (aside from an obliging mention by that most mysterious of figures, Archbishop Ussher of Armagh) before turning up in 1769 at the

English Jesuit College, Liège and then on to Stoneyhurst College, Clitheroe, Lancs in 1794 when the left-footers were allowed back in. There it was proudly displayed alongside a Shakespeare First Folio and a thorn from Jesus' crown of thorns until 2012 when it was purchased by a consortium of British Library, Durham Cathedral and Durham University. Shifts back and forth between sponsoring venues.

3. *The Echternach Gospels*
Created 'presumably in Lindisfarne' around 700. Not used in Northumbria but despatched to Echternach Monastery in Luxembourg just after 700 for use as a gospel book there. Now in the *Bibliothèque nationale*, Paris

4. *The Durham Gospels*
Also created around 700 'presumably in Lindisfarne'. Only fragments have survived. Now in Durham Cathedral library.

5. *Manuscript A.II.10*
Also probably Lindisfarne, also around 700, also in fragments, also in Durham Cathedral Library

Interesting place, Lindisfarne. When I say interesting, I mean uninteresting. It is a thousand acres of the flattest, bleakest, most windswept, most Godawful bit of North Sea coast outside Skegness. It is superior to Skegness only in being cut off from the mainland twice a day by the tide thereby keeping visitor numbers down to the half-million mark even in good years. In the twelfth century Lindisfarne had another geographical advantage: it was sixty-three miles, as the pilgrim walks, from Durham Cathedral. A good workout but worth it, especially after the cathedral authorities built a visitor centre, Lindisfarne Priory, on the island, complete with a marker showing where St Cuthbert had originally been buried five centuries before in 678 AD. As he was currently interred in Durham Cathedral itself this made for a particularly satisfying there-and-back. There were the usual 'brochures', manuscripts explaining the background for the lay audience, in memorable detail, and rendered in a suitably olden days style to enhance the visitor experience.

The operation was conducted by the Benedictine Order who, on top of their religious and administrative duties, were the Thomas Cooks of the twelfth century. On the domestic front they were in charge of Durham Cathedral, Lindisfarne Priory, Jarrow and Wearmouth monasteries (and some thirty other British ecclesiastical complexes) and they also prefigured Thomas Cook in being Europe-wide. One of their twelfth century pilgrim packages was centred on Echternach which is still, to this day, Luxembourg's premier tourist attraction. (No sniggering.) What the twelfth century Benedictines might or might not have been aware of was the connection between Northumberland and Luxembourg five hundred years earlier

> **The Echternach Gospels (Paris, Bib. N., MS. lat. 9389)
> were produced, presumably at Lindisfarne Abbey in
> Northumbria, around the year 690. The scribe of the
> Durham Gospels is believed to have created the
> Echternach Gospels**

This is spooky. For twelfth century Benedictine monks to possess two very ancient School of Northumbria manuscripts is remarkable, for the two manuscripts to have been written *by the same person* is incredible. To appreciate the true dimensions of the coincidence will require something alien to manuscript scholars: probability theory. This is the situation as historians understand it

1. A large number of manuscripts were produced in Western Europe during the period 400–1000 AD
2. Due to the random vicissitudes of history only a small number of these manuscripts have survived to the present day
3. All things being equal, the probability that two of these surviving manuscripts would be written by the same scribe is vanishingly small
4. If all things are not equal, for example if two surviving manuscripts shared a common provenance, and hence parallel rather than random vicissitudes of history, that probability rises from 'vanishingly small' to 'small but not vanishingly small'
5. The Echternach Gospels and the Durham Gospels were written *c* 700 by the same scribe
6. However they have *completely different provenances* – the

first started life in north-east England but was immediately taken to Luxembourg and later to Paris, the second started life in north-east England and stayed there

7. The chances of them both surviving are therefore vanishingly small
8. Since they have, the probability they are manuscripts written in Europe during the period 400–1000 AD is vanishingly small.

A more plausible scenario, though the probability of modern scholars agreeing with it is vanishingly small, would be

1. A limited number of manuscripts were produced in twelfth century Europe to resemble manuscripts of c 400–1000 AD
2. A fair proportion of these have survived
3. All things being equal the probability of two of them being by the same author is fair to middling
4. If two of them have a shared common history, for instance if they were both created in the same Benedictine scriptorium for the Benedictine pilgrimage trade, the probability rises from fair to middling to middling to good.

If you prefer your history to be middling-to-good, you might care to join me for a trip to Luxembourg to discover why a twelfth century gospel book made to look like a seventh century gospel book found its way from Durham to Echternach (or vice versa). Whichever way round it was, the Benedictines were tasked with spreading gospel book techniques from one place to the other. Academic historians agree the transfer took place and that the transfer was highly significant, but place these events five hundred years earlier and for a very different purpose

> **This location was very significant for the production of Insular manuscripts, such as the Durham Gospels (ms. A.II.17) and the Lindisfarne Gospels (ms. Cotton Nero D. IV). The Echternach Gospels, and other such Hiberno-Saxon codices, were highly important instructional devices used in the eighth century onwards primarily for conversion**

I cannot myself imagine waving a foreign language book about would convert many eighth century pagans though I do concur the Echternach

Gospels was a 'highly important instructional device'. We may not be able to agree on time or motive but can we at least agree the *Echternach Gospels* played as central a part in Luxembourg Christianity as, say, the *Cuthbert Gospels* did in northern England? If so, we shall have to identify Luxembourg's St Cuthbert

> The Echternach Gospels were probably taken by St. Willibrord (c. 658 – 7 November 739 AD), a Northumbrian missionary, to his newly founded Echternach Abbey in Luxembourg, from which they are named

We must first conduct our due diligence background check – the archaeology. The results have come back positive! Or to use the jargon term, negative. There is nothing of the right age to be found at Echternach, just as there was nothing to be found at Lindisfarne. Nevertheless there is a profound difference between the two sites. Lindisfarne is, with the best will in the world, rather off the beaten track and its pre-1100 archaeology consists of a farmstead or two. Echternach by contrast is on an all too often beaten track

> With its Merovingian, Roman and Gothic style elements this church built on an ancient Roman castellum is worth a visit. Interestingly, there is a Roman fountain inside the church

It is not as if they do not know where to look. But Luxembourgeois archaeology may not be as well-developed as our own so we shall have to turn to history proper for the answers. Unfortunately Luxembourgeois history may not be as well-developed as our own

> The Abbey was founded by St Willibrord, the patron saint of Luxembourg, in the 7th century. For three hundred years, it benefited from the patronage of a succession of rulers, and was the most powerful institution in Luxembourg

No disrespect to Luxembourg but three centuries as a powerhouse is stretching the facts to their uttermost

> The early 9th century was the heyday of the abbey, as it enjoyed power, both spiritual and temporal. However, this was all guaranteed only by the Carolingians. When

> the authority of the centralised Frankish state collapsed during the civil wars under Louis the Pious, so too did the power of the abbey. In 847, the Benedictine monks were ejected and replaced by lay-abbots

This is the bit they cannot find. The bit they can find is

> The fortunes of the abbey continued to vary with the fortunes of the Holy Roman Empire. When Otto the Great reunited the Empire, he sought to rejuvenate the intellectual and religious life of his dominions, including Echternach. In 971, he restored the Benedictines to Echternach with forty monks of that order from Trier. The abbey entered a second Golden Age, as it once again became one of northern Europe's most influential abbeys

Well, no, it turns out they *would* have been able to find the Golden Age building but for an inopportune disaster

> The imposing Romanesque Basilica has a long and moving history. Its crypt houses the tomb of the only saint buried in Luxembourg, Saint Willibrord. It was originally built in 700 but destroyed by a big fire in 1031

They got the body out in time but alas the building itself was destroyed with such finality that nothing can be found pre-1031. Even 1031 is not set in stone. The Luxembourg government has adopted a more nuanced position

> In the 10th and 12th century, a three-nave church was built and equipped with Gothic elements in 1480. The frescoed church was rebuilt and restored several times

Just because there are intangible aspects to Willibrord's abbey has not prevented the wider world doffing its cap

> The famous Dancing Procession of Echternach became part of UNESCO'S Intangible World Cultural Heritage in 2010

There is nothing intangible though about Willibrord, he is Luxembourg's one and only saint. Uh-oh! Somebody else has put in a claim

Willibrord (Latin: *Villibrordus*) was a Northumbrian missionary saint, known as the "Apostle to the Frisians" in the modern Netherlands. He became the first Bishop of Utrecht

This is before Benelux so they'll have to get a shift on

In 698, Irmina of Oeren granted the Northumbrian missionary Willibrord land at Echternach to build a larger monastery, appointing Willibrord as abbot. In part, the choice was due to Willibrord's reputation as a talented proselytiser (he is known as the Apostle to the Frisians), and, in part, due to the danger posed to his see of Utrecht by pagan Frisian raiders

Frisians raiding Frisia, there's a turn-up for the books. Some other book. The Vikings may have changed their name but not their spots so, whether it is Lindisfarne or Utrecht, Vikings or Frisians, there is nothing for it but to saddle up and move out. Luxembourg is a good bit inland so, we are told, provided safe haven for Willibrord over the next forty years

Willibrord died on 7 November 739 at the age of 81, and according to his wish, was buried in Echternach. He was quickly judged to be a saint

But now, on the orthodox timeline, something rather unexpected ensued. As reported, the chief problem then was that everybody was pagan and the chief concern was getting them converted. It seems not. What eighth century Luxembourgers really wanted were *decent pilgrimage opportunities*

Willibrord was interred in the oratory, which soon became a place of pilgrimage

and they demanded all those day trips that became so popular later in the High Middle Ages

Willibrord wells, which skirted his missionary routes, were visited by the people, to solicit the healing of various nervous diseases, especially of children

Of course the one thing needed to keep the show on the road, whether it is eighth century, twelfth century or twenty-first century, is

91

St Willibrord himself and what with one thing and another he is not always available to view. Fancy sepulchres are all very well but opening and closing them can be a logistical nightmare. If you don't believe me, you can check it out for yourself, it's still there, in Echternach, Willibrord tucked up safely inside. But if the body isn't available on the day, you could always kiss his gospel book because that's still there too. Not exactly *there*, it's in Paris, and you may not be allowed to kiss it – health and safety – but the point is *Willibrord lives*! The dance goes on.

✳   ✳   ✳

None of this settles the question of where the *Echternach Gospels* was created. Whether it is genuine seventh century or forged twelfth century, it is as likely to be a Luxembourg production as a Durham one; everything might continue to be going east to west, seventh century or twelfth century. Our doubts over the Lindisfarne and Cuthbert Gospels do not help either, they too might have been written/forged in either place. We are down to our last two candidates but, to our great good fortune, these will finally, once and for all, tell us whether the tide has turned

> *The Durham Gospels* Only fragments of this gospel book survive which are now in the Durham Cathedral library

> *Manuscript A.II.10* Only fragments of this gospel book survive which are now in the Durham Cathedral library

This is our first encounter with 'fragments' – all the gospel books so far have been more or less complete. 'Fragments' present something of an enigma as, whatever else gospel books were, they were always highly valued objects. They can be lost through accidental happenstance, they can lose a few pages in dubious circumstance, but how can they be lost *mostly*? The explanation is *duh*, they were not gospel books in the first place. The Durham Gospels and Manuscript A. II.10 are not even two objects. They are not one object. They are not objects at all. They are *work product*.

Durham was a twelfth century 'forgery factory' producing material for a variety of purposes. For them, gospels books were all in a day's work. Not very many days at that. To us post-Gutenberg types (I'll leave the pun in) manuscripts always appear to be works of inordinate and expensive labour. In practice they can be turned out by trained scribes with ease – and not by expensive Latin-trained monks either, the only scientifically identified gospel book scribes were women, as we shall see in the next chapter. Even such lavishly illustrated productions as the *Lindisfarne Gospels* or the *Book of Kells*, which we habitually regard as incredibly painstaking works of high art, are just painterly dudes doodling. I'll leave that pun in as well because if one looks at these convoluted 'Celtic' curlicues not as an art connoisseur, not as an art historian, but as an art cynic, it will be immediately recognised the complexity is *not* designed to say to the viewer "Look at me, don't I excite your Christian devotion?" but "Look at me, aren't I exquisitely and expensively produced?" It is certainly true the *Lindisfarne Gospels* and the *Book of Kells* are high-end fine art, so is a van Eyck knock-off. It is also true the illustrations in gospel books were very expensive to produce but then again pilgrimages and real estate are very profitable enterprises. So are van Eyck knock-offs.

We cannot say precisely what the 'Durham fragments' represent. This particular 'work product' really does cover a multitude of sins. Take your pick

> exemplars for learner-scribes
> early attempts by learner-scribes
> gospel book commissions never paid for
> spares for new commissions
> spares from old commissions
> obsolete pages in the ever-evolving task of keeping up with
>   changes in Biblical exegetics

or add your own. The central point is that while factories export finished goods, *work product stays at home*. This is how we know the movement is Durham–Echternach not Echternach–Durham.

But when? We are at odds with the academics – seventh century or twelfth century – but this too can be resolved by the simple observation that this illicit work-product *has survived*. It shows at the very least a degree of insouciance on the part of people engaged in what are criminal activities by any standards. Except twelfth century standards

There is a cloud of witness that forgery was regarded
as a very heinous crime in the twelfth century. None
the less, it was also entirely respectable. The twelfth
century seems to be regarded by historians, certainly
by Brooke, as the great age of forgery encompassing
in his words 'the early privileges and charters of
almost every European country'. He also points out
that forgers of seals and documents were clerics
and therefore exempt from physical punishment/
mutilations (unlike secular forgers e.g. of coins)

But does 'respectable' mean *legal*? Passing off forgeries as the real thing
may be doing God's work but it is still against the law of the land. Unless
you were the law of the land

**The County Palatine of Durham was an area in the
North of England that was controlled by the** Bishop of
Durham

and they had the documentation to prove it

**The territory was originally the Liberty of Durham
under the control of the Bishop of Durham. The
liberty was also known variously as the "Liberty of St
Cuthbert's Land", "The lands of St. Cuthbert between
Tyne and Tees" or "The Liberty of Haliwerfolc". The
bishops' special jurisdiction was based on claims
that King Ecgfrith of Northumbria had granted a
substantial territory to St Cuthbert on his election
to the see of Lindisfarne in 684. In about 883, a
cathedral housing the saint's remains was established
at Chester-le-Street and Guthfrith, King of York,
granted the community of St Cuthbert the area
between the Tyne and the Wear. In 995 the see was
moved again to Durham**

But could they make it stick? Who are these southern softies coming up
to mix it with our friends in the north? Oh no! It's the best-equipped,
most centrally-organised, most militarily-proficient army in Europe!

Following the Norman invasion, **the administrative
machinery of government was only slowly extended
to northern England. In the twelfth century a shire or**

**county of Northumberland was formed, and Durham
was considered to be within its bounds**

What chance did a mere bishop have against the oncoming, all-conquering Norman military machine? There were clearly no prospects manning the barricades, could chances be improved manning the scriptoria?

**However the authority of the sheriff of
Northumberland and his officials was disputed
by the bishops. The crown still regarded Durham
as falling within Northumberland until the late
thirteenth century. Matters came to a head in 1293
when the bishop and his steward failed to attend
proceedings of quo warranto held by the justices
of Northumberland. The bishop's case was heard
in Parliament, where he stated that Durham lay
outside the bounds of any English shire and that
"from time immemorial it had been widely known
that the sheriff of Northumberland was not sheriff of
Durham nor entered within that liberty as sheriff ...
nor made there proclamations or attachments"**

Good try, bish, but nobody's going to be convinced by that kind of ancient mumbo jumbo. Oh, they were

**The arguments appear to have been accepted, as by
the fourteenth century Durham was accepted as a
liberty which received royal mandates direct. In effect
it was a private shire, with the bishop appointing his
own sheriff. The area eventually became known as the
"County Palatine of Durham"**

Forgery was not war by other means. The Durham situation came about because of geography, military technology and the then political facts of life. Scotland is a lot nearer than London, so the locals had to be a bulwark against the Scots without being a bulwark against London. All states of the High Middle Ages had to solve the problem of protecting their distant borders with forces strong enough to do the job without those same forces being centres of instability for the state as a whole. Each medieval state came up with solutions with greater or lesser success. Indeed, medieval history (not to mention Shakespeare's history plays) are largely a record of how it was done, or not done. The English had four such problems and solved them in four different ways: the Welsh marcher lords, the Pale of Settlement around Dublin, a professional garrison at Calais and the Palatine of Durham. The ecclesiastical establishment in Durham had made sure their preferred solution was the one adopted for the Scottish borders. Forgery was politics by other means.

Chapter 6

The Lichfield Gospels

The first crack in the received wisdom of English Dark Age history occurred in 2003 when workmen making repairs under the nave of Lichfield Cathedral dug up a carved angel with flecks of paint on it. It had an uncanny resemblance to an angel in the *Lichfield Gospels*, an eighth century illuminated manuscript. The concordance became definitive when it was found the paint colour matched up too. The conclusion was inescapable: the Lichfield Gospels were created in Lichfield. That may not surprise you but it certainly surprised the experts. Until then the Lichfield Gospels had simply been regarded as an example of a well-understood genre, produced in various places, none anywhere near Lichfield

> No pre-Norman Conquest text or manuscript, teacher or scholar can be linked without question to Lichfield ... The cathedral's sole pre-Conquest manuscript, the illuminated 8th-century gospel book known as the Lichfield Gospels, did not originate at Lichfield. It was probably produced in Ireland, Iona, or Northumbria ... It was in Wales by the early 9th century and came to Lichfield only in the 10th century

Eighth century illuminated gospel books are the signature product of the 'Celtic Revival' which stretched from Ireland through Iona to Lindisfarne, from there to Echternach, and onwards through Europe. The notion they were *also* being created in a notoriously philistine Anglo-Saxon kingdom in the English midlands was so unforeseen the historians had no alternative but to carefully ignore it. There must be a misinterpretation. English Dark Age history was not about to be rewritten because of some tomfoolery about workmen, angels and flecks of paint. Call the whole thing 'inconclusive' and kick it into the long grass for peer review.

The crack became a fissure in 2014 when a visiting American academic, armed with the bells and whistles the British view with caution, examined the *Lichfield Gospels* using Reflectance Transformation Imaging. He discovered the scribes responsible for the book had written their names in it and they turned out to be both Anglo-Saxon and women. The accepted view of Celtic monks creating these fabulous works of art on remote islets was so fractured the historians were forced into action. They agreed the *Lichfield Gospels* had been written in Lichfield, now only the implications had to be carefully ignored. In fact, looked at in the proper light, it was *good* news. Mercians composing eighth century illustrated gospel books may be a smidgeon anomalous but it was, when all's said and done, only what other Anglo-Saxons were doing over in Northumbria. The Ionan Movement had obviously spread further than anyone had hitherto suspected. This comfortable and comforting conclusion was shattered by a sequence of events, starting in the spring of 2016, when the matter came to the attention of a fearless, dynamic, stridently anti-academic polymath with a brain the size of a house, and he told me.

This was the fly in the soothing balm

It was in Wales by the early ninth century and came to Lichfield only in the tenth century

The book had always started life, vaguely but safely, in Ireland, Iona, Northumbria, any damned place *except Lichfield* – because the new adjusted provenance of the Lichfield Gospels now read

The *Lichfield Gospels* was made in Lichfield in the eighth century, was in Wales during the ninth century and back in Lichfield in the tenth century

It is not normal behaviour to produce a magnificent work of art, keep it for a century, send it off to a foreign country for a century, and then have them send it back. So an elegant shrug was adopted, "This is the Dark Ages, nobody really knows for sure what was going on; if that's what happened, that's what happened." A more Occamite itinerary *was* available

The *Lichfield Gospels* was made in Lichfield in the eighth century, stayed in Lichfield during the ninth century, and was still in Lichfield in the tenth century and that would have satisfied English Dark Age historians. If that's what happened, that's what happened. It would only be *Welsh* Dark Age historians who would be discomfited because the Lichfield Gospels' sojourn in Wales is very, very important to Welsh history.

The *Lichfield Gospels* is known to the Welsh as the *Llandeilo Gospels* because their manuscript specialists have always believed the book spent those hundred years in Llandeilo, a smallish town at the end of the Brecon Beacons. The reason they believe this is because it contains (but of course) ninth century land charters dealing with monastic property in and around Llandeilo, Carmarthenshire. More to the point, these charters are the earliest, and only contemporary, evidence of how the Welsh recorded their land ownership. We may be losing track of all the monks in all the parts of the British Isles putting land charters into gospel books, so we had better have a table

Nationality of charters	Name of Gospel Book	Date of Gospel Book	Date earliest charter entered
English	Gospels of St Augustine	sixth century	tenth century
Irish	Book of Kells	eighth century	eleventh century
Welsh	Lichfield Gospels	eighth century	ninth century

Carmarthenshire monks of the ninth century had no known connection with either tenth century Kentish monks or eleventh century Irish monks but when it comes to bizarre practices, what does it matter whether they were independently invented once, twice, thrice. Put it down to zeitgeist (don't send that out for peer review).

Even so, there were grave problems of transmission. Not of the idea that gospel books were good places for registering land charters but of the physical transmission of the *Lichfield Gospels* itself. Anonymous gospel books are ideal vehicles for any number of fell purposes but they have to stay anonymous if they are to fool anybody – and that includes modern academics. Thanks to spectroscopic pigment analysis and reflectance transformation imaging, the *Lichfield Gospels* was no longer

99

anonymous. Imagine what medieval pilgrims would have made of the *Gospels of St Augustine* if Doris and Marge had signed the picture of the Last Supper. Well, they had signed the Lichfield Gospels so what were modern academics to make of that?

Careful ignoral is effective just so long as the wider world is also ignoring the problem. The Welsh would not be ignoring, carefully or otherwise, their Llandeilo Gospels because, it so happens, the Lichfield/Llandeilo Gospels is now the only early gospel book with *a known origin*. Along with the World's Longest Railway Station Name, the Welsh could lay claim to a share in the World's Earliest Extant Manuscript With A Known Origin. Time for another table.

Gospel Book	Proposed Origin	Reason given
Codex Sinopensis	Syria, Palestine or possibly Mesopotamia	Illustration style
Gospels of St Augustine	Rome or Monte Cassino have been suggested	Uncial writing
Book of Kells	Disputed, probably Iona	Academic opinion
Cuthbert's Gospel	Jarrow, Monkwearmouth or Lindisfarne	Circumstantial
Echternach Gospels	Jarrow, Monkwearmouth or Lindisfarne	Historical sources
Lichfield Gospels	Lichfield	Scientific analysis

In general, early gospel books can be moved around without having to be too specific, but the Lichfield book was now officially written *at Lichfield*; it went *to Llandeilo*; it arrived back *at Lichfield*. If early Welsh history was to be supported with textual evidence, some very specific reasons for these very specific jouneyings would have to be produced. By hook or by crook. The first hurdle, getting the *c* 700 Gospels out of Lichfield in time to get the *c* 800 Llandeilo charters inserted, could be negotiated easily enough. Vikings. The Vikings had landed at the Wirral on the Mercian coast at more or less the right date so what would be more natural for Lichfield monks than to take their precious gospel

100

book off to somewhere safer. Alternatives were no doubt canvassed but Winchester, York, London, any English refuge capable of standing up to Vikings, was just as capable of standing up to Lichfield, would they give this expensive work of art back when the coast was clear? Which is possibly why the foreign but inconsequential Llandeilo was selected instead. What the Mercian Antiquities Preservation Service could not have known – because English Anglo-Saxon monks only hit on the idea of putting charters in gospel books in the tenth century (see table) – was that the Llandeilo monks would hit on this idea in the ninth century (see table) and start putting *their* land charters in *Lichfield's* gospel book! The cheek! But worse than that, these Welsh monks now had an even better reason for not returning the book to Lichfield. It contained things far more precious to them than the actual book, their land charters. But they did! If that's what happened, that's what happened.

✶   ✶   ✶

The *Lichfield Gospels* is not in itself of great interest, which is doubtless why it is now in Lichfield Cathedral rather than national collections in Cambridge, London or Dublin. It should though by rights be in the national collection in Cardiff because

> **The manuscript includes, as marginalia, some of the earliest known examples of written Old Welsh, dating to the early part of the eighth century**

Goodness, it's another case of triple independent invention! Like Anglo-Saxon monks coming up with the first written demotic for a thousand years, like Irish monks coming up with the first written demotic for a thousand years, we now have Welsh monks coming up with the first written demotic for a thousand years. They were as usual doing all this unbeknownst to one other but we can leave the Guinness people to sort out who got there first, second and third. We are focused on the land charters, not the language they were written in. Time for another potted history (Wales, with special reference to the recording of land holdings). Do not confuse potted with potty

Year dot

–50 AD *Prehistoric Period.* Nothing known about land ownership

50–400 *Roman Period.* Land ownership as dictated by the Romans

400–1066 *Age of Saints.* Wales is a congeries of petty states ruled by princes. The whole is held together by charismatic Christian preachers ('the Saints') starting with St David. This combination of theocracy and temporality might be unusual but it was apparently cohesive enough to keep Wales more or less free from foreign occupation, notably Anglo-Saxons and Vikings, for six hundred years. Land is assumed to be held by the standard mix of tradition and force plus, curiously, several hundred land charters. There is no record of the kind of legal apparat normally required to superintend this sort of formal property registration – possibly eisteddfodau were pressed into service – but there are records of the land charters themselves. Some are in the ninth century Llandeilo Gospels, now in Lichfield Cathedral, others are known from twelfth century copies in cartularies, now in the National Library of Wales, Cardiff. This is true not just about land holding registration, *everything* known about the early history of Wales – the saints, the princes, the poets – can be gleaned only from either twelfth century copies or the Lichfield Gospels. Which is why Welsh Dark Age historiographers whisper among themselves, "If *that's* a forgery, Dai, look you, we'll have to fall back on hwyl." Hwyl is the Welsh acronym for The National Library of Wales.

1066–1169 *Norman Period.* The Normans mainly leave the Welsh alone apart from busying themselves setting up a chain of monasteries along a corridor roughly corresponding to the present A40, from Gloucester in England to St David's at the southwestern-most tip of Wales. St David's, the single most inaccessible place in the whole country, is adopted as the ecclesiastical capital of Wales, not because

102

of any strategic considerations on the part of foreigners. but because it was the sixth century birthplace of St David, the patron saint of Wales. This is confirmed by an extensive body of literature from the sixth century onwards. Which has disappeared but must have lasted until the twelfth century because we have twelfth century versions.

1169 The Normans (now technically Angevins) invade Ireland, setting out from St David's with a logistic supply line running via a series of monasteries along what is now the A40. These monasteries have documentation demonstrating that, far from being some kind of alien Norman intrusion, they are the natural successors of the 'claes' (singular 'clas'), proto-monasteries founded by 'the Saints' during the period 400–1000 AD. It further transpires that the extensive landholdings of these Norman monasteries were originally, freely, legally, even enthusiastically, donated to the *claes* by pious people during this period and therefore it is only right and proper that the Norman monasteries should inherit the land as well. This is all recorded not just in land charters but many other sources, notably the Lives of these various saints. It is true the sources are all from the twelfth century but they are based on 'earlier material'. Although we do not now have access to *any* of this earlier material, it would be incorrect to conclude they were all made up in the twelfth century as this would imply the saints were all made up too and that Christianity arrived in Wales in the twelfth century courtesy of the 'English' which is not the case.

1169– present day The Norman stroke Angevin stroke Plantagenet stroke Tudor stroke some non-Welsh dynasties' view of land management was extended to the whole of Wales. Apply to the Land Registry in Swansea for information regarding your own claim on Welsh real estate.

* * *

But that is the wider picture, our own area of study is limited to the
Lichfield stroke Llandeilo Gospels. Or, as the town soon became known,
Llandeilo Fawr ('the Great'). Whether the tag was acquired, as Welsh
historians believe, because early Saints favoured the town, or because
Llandeilo controls a key strategic position where the A40 crosses the
River Towy, is debatable. The orthodox view does have the merit of
some presumed historical evidence

> The material prosperity of the community was assured
> by its acquisition of land. The marginal notes in the
> Lichfield Gospels are one source of information here,
> while Geoffrey and Urban of Llandaff in the early
> twelfth century seem to have had access to a collection
> of charters originally brought together at Llandeilo
> Fawr, and from which they added suitably amended
> versions to the Book of Llandaff

The *Book of Llandaff* is the chief twelfth century cartulary containing
copies of the 'hundreds of early Welsh land charters', of which we
have already spoken, and for which there are no extant originals other
than the ones in the Lichfield Gospels. Thus Llandeilo uniquely and
fortunately had a double lock for its land: the charters recorded in the
Lichfield Gospels in the ninth century and the copies recorded in the
Book of Llandaff in the twelfth century. And how fortunate Llandeilo
was to have its original charters because the Book of Llandaff is not
necessarily to be relied on

> The book was compiled from a pre-existing collection
> of nine charter groups, originally entered in Gospel
> Books, and appears to have been produced to help in
> Bishop Urban's diocesan boundary disputes with the
> dioceses of St David's and Hereford. Many of the
> supposed early charters have therefore been 'edited' to
> serve Llandaff's interests. They are also undated and
> many are corrupt

Not to mention bogus from start to finish but I suppose a sinner come to partial judgement is better than not at all. However, since Llandeilo alone has the *Lichfield Gospels*, it really ought to have its very own niche in the National Library of Wales archives. The town's official origins are

> **Llandeilo is named after one of the better-known Celtic saints of the 6th century, Saint Teilo. The Welsh word *llan* signified a monastery or a church. Saint Teilo, who was a contemporary of Saint David, the patron Saint of Wales, established a small monastic settlement (*clas*) on the site of the present-day parish church. Although there is very little factual detail about the life of Saint Teilo, it appears that he was highly respected in his lifetime, and revered after his death: there are 45 places dedicated to him, some as far afield as Cornwall and Brittany**

Memo to Cardiff archivist: file under R for Rubbish. *Llan* does not signify 'a monastery or a church', it means 'a place, an enclosure, a defended settlement' and is merely the Welsh equivalent of comparable European suffixes denoting the same thing: –ton in England, –burgh in Scotland, –burg in Germany, –ville in France. *Deilo* does not refer to St Teilo, it refers to

> **teilo, teilio:** soil; to spread dung (on); manure, cover with dung or manure

Llandeilo means a place where animals are aggregated, whether for security, for fattening, for buying, for selling, for breeding with prized stock. So you will have to choose between

1. There are forty-five places in Wales (and linguistically cognate areas in Cornwall and Brittany) which are all named after a saint for whom there is 'very little factual detail' or
2. There are forty-five livestock markets in Wales (and linguistically cognate areas in Cornwall and Brittany).

Early Wales was either a land of saints or a land of sheep – or both – but like everywhere else in Europe at the time, it was also a land requiring 'enclosed settlements' for all manner of purposes. There are something like three hundred and fifty place names in Wales beginning with *Llan* and according to place-name theorists they are named after saints. These saints are, for the most part, even less well documented than the very little factually known St Teilo – some have no independent existence outside the place names, which is kind of circular – but a good many are apparently named for extremely famous saints. *Llanfair f*or example is not 'the place where a fair is held'. Not at all, it is the 'Church of St Mary'. The place-name people believe the Welsh keep on getting the name of the second most famous person in the world wrong.

Be that as it may, we are concerned with St Teilo who is said to have set up a monastery in the sixth century at a place now known as Llandeilo in the county of Carmarthenshire. The coincidence between saint's name and town name can be variously explained

1. The town of Llandeilo derives its name from being the site of a *clas* founded by a holy man called Teilo
2. "St Teilo" was invented by monks at a Norman monastery established at Llandeilo in Carmarthenshire to justify their ownership of extensive land holdings given, they claimed, hundreds of years before by Welsh devotees to support a previous monastery founded by the said Teilo, the eponymous saint of the town.
3. Teilo's mum was a fan of Johnny Cash and named him Dung Enclosure

✶   ✶   ✶

However much the written record is distrusted, the archaeology never lies and we know, as it were, where the archaeology lies

St Teilo established a small monastic settlement (*clas*) on the site of the present-day parish church

I am obliged to report that so far no pre-1100 ecclesiastical archaeology in, around, under, within miles of, the present-day parish church has been found. But, as we know, this is also in the *Book of Llandaff* so perhaps we might have better luck with the archaeology of Llandaff. There will assuredly be no shortage this time because

The Cathedral Church of SS Peter & Paul, Dyfrig, Teilo and Euddogwy is the mother church of the Diocese of

> Llandaff ... [which] ... takes its name from the ancient
> cathedral that was established on the site of a church
> built by the Celtic saints in the 6th century... [it] stands
> on one of the oldest Christian sites in Britain

We will have to rely on the archaeology because not much is to be seen above ground

> Nothing remains of the original church but a Celtic
> Cross that stood nearby can still be seen near the door
> of the [thirteenth century] Chapter House

Ye olde crosses always survive a lot longer than ye olde churches they stood beside but what of ye olde archaeology?

> Despite the archaeological potential of the application
> area, the watching brief identified limited archaeological
> remains within the area of observed groundworks and
> no artefactual material was recovered

Not a lot of point keeping watch there, but if this is the main seat of a diocese there will be a bishop's palace somewhere close by

> Thought to have been first constructed in late C13,
> substantially intact c.1600, the palace/castle decayed
> thereafter. The castle/palace is the only surviving
> residence of the medieval clergy of Llandaff

But at least there is some archaeology

> Finds dating to the Neolithic were dug up in 2014 and
> a beaker of the early Bronze Age was found by accident
> under a house.

Good, good. Anything Roman? Anything Dark Age? Anything?

> ... a small excavation also took place on week day
> evenings at the Bishop's Palace in Llandaff although
> little of note was found due to the major part of the site
> being covered by allotments

Don't mess with allotment holders in the land of the leek. On the other hand one is entitled to be a bit sniffy about Welsh archaeologists' somewhat lacklustre efforts investigating 'one of the oldest Christian sites in Britain'. Have they been more on the ball elsewhere in the vicinity?

In other aspects, the pre-existing dataset was very poor. The research audit for the area noted that there were only thirty sites of the category 'Religious, ritual and funerary' for the Early Medieval period [400 - 1000 AD] in the SMR [Sites and Monument Record]

Only thirty sites. The dataset was very poor. In archaeology there are various ways of delivering bad news about the paucity of archaeology:

inconclusive
yet to be fully understood
requires a fuller and more comprehensive excavation
results as yet await publication
the original excavators have died and their research notes are lost

To come right out and say 'poor' is pretty drastic and tantamount to saying 'practically nothing'. 'Very poor' means 'a bit less than practically nothing'.

Archaeologists are a sturdy breed, out there in the broiling sun, and are never for one moment downhearted by lack of results. They can always gerrymander what they have. When confronted with the Dark Ages, Welsh archaeologists glide effortlessly between post-Roman, Dark Age, Early Medieval and Medieval. First priority is to demonstrate that not finding much is not for want of trying on their part. 'Only thirty sites' might suggest less than optimal enthusiasm but appearances can be deceiving

This was partly due to the conflation of material of this period under a general 'Medieval' period heading (Evans et al 2002, 141-2), but also because in most cases the fact that a church had been mentioned in the Book of Llandaff was merely noted as part of its general description as a monument of the Medieval period. As a result of the additions and modifications made during the course of the project, there are now 223 sites

Thirty has become two hundred and twenty-three. Discovered in the Book of Llandaff rather than under the ground but it rains a lot in Wales so there can be no objection to indoor archaeology.

The correction of the period field from 'Medieval' to 'Early Medieval', accounts for 131 of these entries, but 92 are completely new entries, 74 of them resulting from the systematic examination of documentary sources and the addition to the database of those ecclesiastical establishments whose location is known or can be inferred

Oh no, it's going back down and still all from historical sources. Please, surely, there must be *some* archaeology?

The other main lacuna is in excavation. Only fourteen sites excavated under modern conditions have produced structural evidence definitely or probably relating to the period. Of these, three were entirely settlement sites and at another three, evidence for the period consisted only of limited traces of activity, whose nature is not necessarily clear, found during the excavation of earlier sites. The remainder are almost entirely burials; there is very little evidence of any structures associated with ecclesiastical activity

I think they mean 'a bit less than practically nothing'. Or a bit less.

*   *   *

But we keep getting sidetracked. This chapter is on the *Lichfield Gospels*, otherwise the *Llandeilo Gospels*, and we shall need to know about the fortunes of Llandeilo. What reports do we have of developments after St Teilo's foundation in the sixth century?

By the 8th century Llandeilo Fawr was the centre of a bishopric and probably the mother church of a large area in what is now north-eastern Carmarthenshire. The church would have been an important landowner and this tradition certainly continued into later medieval times

Probably. Would have. Traditionally. Certainly. But for how long?

Llandeilo lost something of its ecclesiastical importance between 900 and 1200AD. In the ninth century it was the seat of a bishop. By 1200 it was a

> parish church, but with a very extensive parish
> covering some 20,000 acres

An odd – and a dangerous – situation. Twenty thousand acres, even twenty thousand Welsh acres, is a lot for a parish church. Too much, the real estate vultures were circling

> Llandeilo was also a wealthy parish, but its revenues,
> together with the lands of the old Teilo community,
> were transferred to the abbey of Talley in the twelfth
> century

Just like that. As St Thomas Cooper of Caerphilly later remarked. Might we have the name of these holy interlopers?

> Talley Abbey was a monastery of the Premonstratensians, an
> order with a constitution and way of life based on Cistercian
> lines, in the village of Talley in Carmarthenshire, six miles
> north of the market town of Llandeilo

Not one of the majors but the Premonstratensians did have friends in high places

> The order was well supported in England at the end of
> the 12th century. Henry II's chief justiciar, Ranulf de
> Glanville, was prominent among its patrons and it may
> have been this man who influenced Rhys ap Gruffydd,
> the Lord Rhys, in his choice of the Premonstratensians
> for the new house which he founded at Talley in the
> late 1180s, a time of peace and concord between the
> Welsh prince and the English crown

How sweet. What could go possibly wrong?

> The downfall of Ranulf soon afterwards may in turn
> have had some bearing on the fact that no other
> Premonstratensian houses were ever founded in
> Wales, and that Talley was only poorly endowed. Soon
> after its foundation, the canons were involved in an
> extensive lawsuit against the abbot of the neighbouring
> Cistercian house of Whitland, who evidently regarded
> Talley as a dangerous rival

Time to dust off those old land charters. Where the hell did we put them? Oh yes, in the Lichfield Gospels

110

> Memoranda 3 and 4 of the Lichfield Gospels record the gift of some lands and services to the Llandeilo Fawr community c. 850. Memorandum 3 states that Rhys and the 'kindred of Grethi' had given 'to God and St Eliud (Teilo) a place named Trefwyddog (treb guidauc) with food renders from the place, and Memorandum 4 that Rhys and others had given a piece of land, whose boundaries are then described, and with it also were given food renders

That should see off the Cistercians if it stands up in court. But would those blackguards claim the Lichfield Gospels and the charters in it weren't really ninth century at all? No worries on that score, one of the other entries conveniently confirms the whereabouts of the *Lichfield Gospels* at the appropriate time

> It is shown here that Gelhi, the son of Arihtiud, bought this Gospel from Cingal, and gave him for it his best horse; and that for the benefit of his soul he offered this Gospel to God, and on the altar of St. Teilo. †Gelli son of Arihtiud †Cincenn son of Griffith

A horse, a horse, my monastery for a horse. But it's all water under the bridge now. Ancient history. All the monasteries are gone. Dust to dust. Only the *Lichfield Gospels* can tell the world of the greatness that was Llandeilo Fawr.

111

Chapter 7

The Hereford Gospels

Anumber of historians are riveted by the *Hereford Gospels*. Revisionist historians like me mostly. Well, only me to be honest. Everyone else passes over it with disdain as being just one more gospel book. Even its current owners, Hereford Cathedral, treat it as a poor companion to their blessèd Mappa Mundi. This is unfair because, while the origin of the *Hereford Gospels* is hidden in the usual murk, it is at least novel murk

> The Hereford Gospels (**Hereford Cathedral Library, MS P. I. 2**) is an 8th-century **illuminated manuscript gospel book in insular script**. The manuscript was likely produced either in **Wales** or in the **West Country of England**

Hereford is just along the road from Lichfield and Lichfield, we have learned, though neither in Wales nor the West Country, was making eighth century illuminated gospel books. Could there be a connection? Could there be six hundred and fifty connections?

> Correspondences with the Lichfield Gospels include roughly 650 variances from the Vulgate, suggestive that the two manuscripts result from a similar textual tradition

They may not know where the *Hereford Gospels* is from, but they do know where it went

> An added text suggests this was in the **diocese of Hereford in the 11th century**

Have a punt as to what this 'added text' is. No prizes. Land charters. You are clearly in no need of a list of early illuminated gospel books that happen to contain land charters, but we will pop one in for handy reference

Nationality of charters	Name of Gospel Book	Date of Gospel Book	Date Charters Entered
English	Gospels of St Augustine	sixth century	tenth century
Irish	Book of Kells	eighth century	eleventh century
Welsh	Lichfield Gospels	eighth century	ninth century
English	Hereford Gospels	eighth century	eleventh century

The eleventh century charters in the Hereford Gospels can at best only provide a *terminus ante quem* for when the book arrived in Hereford, which might have been centuries earlier if Hereford Cathedral's antecedents are to be believed

> Hereford had become the seat of a **bishopric** as early as the 6th century. In the 7th century the cathedral was refounded by **Putta**. The cathedral of stone, which Milfrid raised, stood for some 200 years, and then, in the reign of **Edward the Confessor** (1042-66), it was altered

Echternach syndrome. What can actually be seen?

> no part of any building earlier than the 11th-century bishop's chapel survives. In 1107 - 48 the cathedral is rebuilt in Norman or Romanesque style. This is the earliest type of architecture still visible in the cathedral today

So a small amount from Edward the Confessor's day but otherwise Norman. The Confessor, being half Anglo-Saxon/ half Norman, left a building that half-survived because the Normans otherwise gave short shrift to Anglo-Saxon ecclesiastical structures. If I had a pound for every time I've heard the phrase "all the Anglo-Saxon churches in England were replaced by Norman ones" I would have enough for a full set of Pevsners. The standard reason given for this dazzling programme of reconstruction is that the Anglo-Saxons built their churches in wood, the Normans in stone. Clearly the Anglo-Saxons had not gone native in the land of Stonehenge. An untutored bystander might conclude there were no Anglo-Saxon churches in the first place. Anyway this does not apply to Hereford Cathedral which had been 'stone for two hundred years' before the Norman builders were on site so no doubt they would have made an exception in its case. But due to a little local difficulty, no decision was required

> Between 1052 and 1056, in the **reign** of Edward the Confessor, Bishop Aethelstan built a new church on the site. The new church was destroyed in 1055 by Griffin King of the Welsh who killed the Cathedral's bishop and many of the clergy

Even the fixtures and fittings were gone

> In 1055 a rebel Welsh army destroyed Athelstan's cathedral; Ethelbert's shrine and many other treasures were lost

But Taffy was a strange thief. He hated historians while retaining a soft spot for historians specialising in eighth century illuminated gospel books

> The destruction of Bishop Aethelstan's minster at Hereford in 1055 was presumably the event which accounts for the almost total absence of records pertaining to the history of the church in the eighth, ninth, tenth and the first half of the eleventh centuries; for although some books did survive (notably the 'Hereford Gospels' and Bishop Aethelstan's evangeliary), it is striking that the sequence of records begins almost pointedly after the 1050's

A historian's worst nightmare, though subsequently Hereford's cathedral became their nicest possible dream

> perhaps uniquely, since the destruction of the cathedral by fire in 1055, the library has suffered no serious depletion by fire, flood, theft or sale of books

which means the two land charters in the *Hereford Gospels* have 'come down to us'. Historians know the date of the first charter because it is kind enough to tell them

> Here it is declared in this document that a shire-meeting sat at Aylton in King Cnut's time

King Cnut (Canute, he of the waves) reigned between 1016 and 1035 so historians confidently date the charter to that time. Pedants might opine, "If someone said they had a penny black made in Queen Victoria's time they would not be saying it during her reign between 1837 and 1901" but they can be reassured on this point because the charter provides corroborating detail from someone who appears to have been present when the charter was originally created

> Thurkil the White stood up in the meeting and asked all the thegns to give his wife the lands unreservedly which her kinswoman had granted her, and they did so

The second charter is more time specific

> The second document, dated 1043-6, records the purchase of some land by Leofwine of Frome, the brother of Leofflaed

These people and their landholdings are exceptionally well recorded in other sources because the people are very famous and because the landholdings were subject to rancorous dispute. Leofflaed is the wife of Thorkill the White, Thorkill's aunt was Lady Godiva, she was the wife of Leofric, Earl of Mercia, and Leofric was for a time the second-most powerful person in England. The holdings were disputed because even being a power in the land did not necessarily make one's estates safe in an era when Anglo-Saxons [Aethelraed the Unready & Co] were replaced by Danes [Canute & Co] who were replaced by Anglo-Saxons [Edward the Confessor & Co] who were replaced by Normans [William the Conqueror & Co] who were replaced by Angevins [Henry II & Co]. Little wonder Thorkill & Co had a family tradition stretching back to Cnut's time of taking the precautionary step of recording their land dealings in ancient gospel books. This too is recorded in one of the *Hereford Gospels* charters

> Then Thurkil rode to St Aethelbert's minster, with the consent and cognisance of the whole assembly and had it recorded in a gospel book

Having acquired the thegns' agreement, it was imperative Thorkill got everything down in writing before they changed their minds

Knock, knock
Who's there?
Thorkill
Thorkill who?
Thorkill the White
Lady Godiva's boy?
Nephew. You're not going to mention...
I'm a man of the cloth. What can I do for you?
I need to register some land.
Certainly. I'll get some parchment. Two groats for the first
page, one groat each continuation page. Cash only, I'm afraid.
Money's no object but I'll be needing something a bit more
secure than a sheet of parchment. I've heard putting land
charters in old manuscripts is the thing to do in these
uncertain times.
I suppose you know your business but I'm afraid I can't help.
The only thing 'old', as you put it, is our illustrated eighth
century Gospel Book.
Proves my point. They always survive. I'd like it registered
in that one, please, if you don't mind.
I most certainly would mind. It's priceless. Our pride and joy.
What do you think scribbling grubby land deals all over two
hundred year old vellum will do for it? On your horse.
You can have half the land.
I'll get the book.

By the time of Domesday Book, Hereford Cathedral
itself held one of the two disputed pieces of land

✳   ✳   ✳

History moves on and historians with it. Slowly, there's no rush. But as
luck would have it there have been some recent developments vis à vis
the Hereford Gospels

A further piece of evidence which has recently come
to light points in the same direction: at least one of
the sheets of parchment that form the pages of the
Hereford Gospels (the bifolium that comprises fols.

116

> 93 and 96) is a palimpsest - that is, it was actually
> prepared for and very probably used in a different
> book, and was subsequently recycled for its present
> context

It is good to hear the eighth century English were doing their bit for the environment but one is entitled to ask, why recycle only one page? There must have been quite a lot of used parchment lying around

> the readiness with which scriptoria recycled
> parchment related rather to two eminently practical
> considerations, namely the ease with which new
> parchment could be manufactured or acquired at the
> centres in question, and the availability or otherwise
> of stocks of decaying or obsolete books whose sheets
> might be reused

Is he suggesting we Brits weren't great readers and had no ready supply of used parchment? Fair point, we do tend to prefer huntin' and fishin'. Not like those swots on the Continent

> The many palimpsests associated with early medieval
> Bobbio, the northern Italian foundation of the
> Irishman Columbanus (d. 615), plainly reflect a lack of
> adequate supplies of new parchment but easy access to
> antiquated manuscripts

Times must have changed since parchment is treated leather and Italy today is regarded as the leather goods capital of the world. There has to be a better explanation for why eighth century Italy was way ahead of us in parchment recycling

> By contrast, in Anglo-Saxon England – whose cool
> damp climate was altogether more favourable for the
> rich pasture essential for nourishing healthy livestock
> with good pelts, and which lacked a reserve of old
> books – palimpsests were extremely rare

See, told you. Outdoor types, us. You might have spotted Bobbio is another major scriptorium founded by peripatetic seventh century Irish monks but I cannot go into that now because, thanks to Brexit, grants for demolishing European history have all but dried up. We must instead hie ourselves off to our local World of Palimpsests emporium

117

> A palimpsest (/ˈpælɪmpsɛst/) is a **manuscript** page, either from a scroll or a book, from which the text has been scraped or washed off so that the page can be reused for another document. Parchment and other materials for writing or engraving upon were expensive to produce, and in the interest of economy were re-used wherever possible

Palimpsests are given a great deal of attention by scholars because modern techniques sometimes allow the previous text to be read and this can be more important than the writing on top

> The Sana'a palimpsest is one of the oldest Qur'anic manuscripts in existence. Carbon dating indicates that the undertext (the scriptio inferior) was written probably within 15 years before the death of the Islamic prophet Muhammad. The undertext differs from the standard Qur'anic text and is therefore the most important documentary evidence for the existence of variant Qur'anic readings

It's OK to carbon date Islamic texts, only Christian ones have to stay safely under lock and key.

Although the manuscript community is enthusiastic about scrutinising what is written on parchment, they are less keen researching the parchment itself. This is not altogether surprising since parchment is a product of the animal skin processing trade and investigating such a disagreeable business does not appeal to your average ivory tower white collar worker. Fortunately this does not apply to me. Not on account of the colour of my collar but because, just as Cockney Londoners are born within the sound of Bow Bells, we estuarine south Londoners are born within the smell of Bermondsey leatherworks, so I am able to pass on the folk wisdom of my birthright.

The skinning of animals and the turning of those skins into useful products is one of the earliest of human accomplishments, going back to the Palaeolithic and beyond. Over thousands of years we've become dab hands. As the skins are by-products of routine meat butchery they are cheap and readily available. However, the skill required to turn untreated skins into useful products does not come cheap and is not readily available; it requires specialists and, as the job is very smelly as

118

well as technically challenging, these specialists tend to be something of a caste apart. Nonetheless they are fully paid-up members of society because their products are not just immensely useful but, before the modern era, there was little in the way of substitutes. So, before the modern era, whenever and wherever human beings were gathered together in appreciable numbers, there was sure to be a leather industry close at hand.

There must then have been a leather industry in England throughout the period 400–1200 AD. But how good were English leather workers when it came to the making of parchment? Television programmes featuring vellum makers (vellum is calfskin parchment) give the impression it is more an arts-and-crafts affair than a job of work, which is certainly the case today when only artists work in vellum. It is less certain this assumption should be projected into the past by historians fondly believing the monkish scribes who wrote on vellum were also the people who made the vellum. This is exceedingly unlikely because vellum production, though routine for leathermakers, would be incredibly difficult, not to say thoroughly uncongenial, for monks. And why would they? Vellum is particularly easy to come by for two reasons

1. In all agricultural communities male calves have little economic value – except for making calfskin products
2. Parchment is flat, one-piece, 'calf-sized' and straightforward to make. Very top quality vellum may not exactly be cheap – it takes a deal of processing to produce a long-lasting, smooth and receptive surface – but it is no different in principle to gloves, shoes, saddles or any other finished goods coming out of the leather industry.

Readily available then to anyone with cash and an ongoing need for parchment, a description that comfortably fits all European monastery scriptoria. Bearing this in mind, let us re-examine the universal belief palimpsests are created because

Parchment and other materials for writing or engraving upon were expensive to produce, and in the interest of economy were re-used wherever possible

Brother Dominic: I'm running out of vellum.
Head of Scriptorium: And you've forgotten where the stationery cupboard is?
Dominic: I've looked. Nothing of the quality I need for this manuscript.
HoS: Oh, all right, you'd better get some more from the suppliers. You may have to order it if it's special grade. Put it on the monastery account.
Dominic: What, in this weather?
HoS: Half an hour in the open air will do you a power of good. You're looking a bit peaky.

Scenario Two

Brother Dominic: I'm running out of vellum.
Head of Scriptorium: And you've forgotten where the stationery cupboard is?
Dominic: I've looked. Nothing of the quality I need for this manuscript.
HoS: Oh very well, you'd better go down to the library and find some book we haven't much use for and tear a page out. Carefully, mind.
Dominic: Won't that ruin the book? Even the old stuff is pretty rare. I thought preserving books was ... you know, one of the reasons we're here.
HoS: Have you seen the price of vellum lately? Once you've got the page removed you'll need to make up an incredibly complex chemical brew and start ever so gently removing the existing words from the page. It's a fiendishly difficult task but I'm sure you'll get the hang of it eventually. When you've done that you'll find you've got a rough surface completely unsuited to writing. Don't worry, now you can make up a second batch of chemicals and start the equally laborious task of smoothing it all out ready for writing on.
Dominic: Blimey O'Reilly, what a palaver.

HoS: Practice makes perfect. But you're not done yet. The page you'll end up with will have a colour and quality quite distinct from all the pages you've been using so far in your manuscript so you'll have to brew up a third batch of chemicals to treat this page so it conforms roughly with all the others. There'll be a lot of hanging around, I'm afraid, because the process involves storing it in controlled conditions for ... well, just keep inspecting it until it looks like all the other pages.

Dominic: The pages I've done already, you mean. What about the next page? And the page after that? I've still got eighty to go.

HoS: Yes, it's a puzzle. The memo from head office was very clear: you must never have more than one or two, three if you're really pushed, of these 'palimpsests' in any single manuscript. I'll have to get back to you on that one. Meanwhile, six months in the tanning salon will do you a power of good. You're looking a bit peaky.

Scenario Three

Abbot: Are you free, brother?

Head of Scriptorium: For you, eminence, always.

Abbot: Got a special job for you. We need to stick a new page into a manuscript.

HoS: Not a problem, we do it all the time.

Abbot: Really, why is that?

HoS: Scribes leave passages out, write them twice, wrong apostle gets drawn ... You can't get the staff. If we had a bigger budget, your eminence...

Abbot: Yes, yes, it's on my list. But this would be an existing manuscript, fairly old.

HoS: That would be more complicated. Haven't got a lot of experience in that line. Might I ask...?

Abbot: No, not at this stage. Can it be done?

HoS: Oh yes, in principle. There'd be a few problems with folio pagination and binding and whatnot but nothing we couldn't handle as long as it's in reasonable condition.

Abbot: Good. And one other thing: it would have to, you know, blend in fairly seamlessly with the existing pages.

HoS: Yes, I see that. Aesthetically, it would be highly desirable. There'd be no trouble with the text. We often have to do new pages by someone else because the original scribe is unavailable. Moved on to pastoral duties for being a bodger generally. It needs a bit of experience and a good eye to reproduce his actual handwriting, that's all. Though in this case maybe a bit more, depending how old this page of yours is.

Abbot: Old. What's the problem now?

HoS: Scribal styles change over the years, uncial, miniscule, you name it. It might require a script these young twerps won't ever have seen. Tell you what, I'll do it myself.

Abbot: Yes, that would be advisable.

HoS: Not a problem. The parchment might be though.

Abbot: What now?

HoS: If this manuscript of yours is old, the parchment will be old and we won't have anything like it for this new page. We don't use anything more than six months old here, it's a point we make to new clients. What we have won't come close to what you'll be needing. Different colour, different texture, different everything.

Abbot: Could you... is it possible to make the new page look, feel, *like* the original, as it were? So as you wouldn't notice.

HoS: Now you're asking. Theoretically I suppose a very good vellum maker could make a passable job of it. It would be a delicate exercise but if you're prepared to spend the money I'm sure it can be arranged.

Abbot: Why don't we do that then? On a strictly confidential basis.

HoS: I definitely would not recommend that.

Abbot: Why not? We're all *brothers* here.

HoS: But vellum makers aren't. The leather trade is clannish and, not to put too fine a point on it, a bit lowlife. This would be in the nature of a very unusual request and would get talked about. If I were you, I wouldn't be putting confidential monastery business in their hands, if you get my drift.

Abbot: Yes, I see that. Let's keep it in-house. Any suggestions?

HoS: There is one way I can see. Parchment might be cheap but scribes' time isn't. We don't like wasting a whole page of text just because of some small error, so one thing we're very good at is scraping off words and putting fresh ones over the top without anyone noticing. Half the time I don't notice it myself. In fact those slipshod little creeps do their best to make sure I don't.

Abbot: Yes, I'm sure you run a tight ship, but how does that solve our problem? I need a complete new page not a re-written old page.

HoS: If we could get a piece of vellum from an existing manuscript of roughly the right age, we could scrape off the existing words and put the new ones on top. Quite a job but if you think it's important enough I think we can come up with something to your specifications.

Abbot: So shall it be.

Did they do a good job in the case of the *Hereford Gospels*?

> **Since the parchment of the manuscript as a whole is yellow in tone and variable in quality, and since the reused sheet has been very thoroughly cleaned, it is barely distinguishable from the rest of the leaves (hence why it has not been recognised hitherto)**

∗   ∗   ∗

It is not just Anglo-Saxon churches the length and breadth of England that have disappeared, Anglo-Saxon archaeology the length and breadth of England has disappeared. Finds are plentiful from the 'Viking Age' AD 900–1100 but not from the 'Anglo-Saxon Age' 500–900. This rum situation occasionally frustrates but never deters archaeologists who know it is there because the historians have told them it is there and while history sits literally on archaeology, historians sit firmly on archaeologists. This one-sided relationship causes difficulties whenever historians are saying one thing and archaeologists are finding another. It requires some *scrambling*. Here are the Top Ten Tips for ensuring the Anglo-Saxon period 500–900 remains forever there but never there

123

1. Take late Anglo-Saxon material and call it early Anglo-Saxon material e.g. Sutton Hoo
2. Take prehistoric structures and call them Anglo-Saxon e.g. Offa's Dyke
3. Claim Anglo-Saxons used perishable materials e.g. wooden churches
4. Claim imperishable things were not much used by early Anglo-Saxons e.g. towns
5. Obfuscate everything by insisting the 'Dark Ages' are 'the Early Medieval period'
6. When necessary describe the 'Early Medieval period' as the 'Dark Ages'
7. Assume Anglo-Saxon is Old English and therefore any old place in England with an English name is ipso facto Anglo-Saxon
8. Count plants in ancient hedgerows; consult botanists re time it takes hedgerow plants to get established – approximately once per hundred years; since there are about fifteen hedgerow plants native to Britain, claim the hedgerows must have been established fifteen hundred years ago, i.e. by Anglo-Saxons
9. Intone the mantra 'The absence of evidence is not evidence of absence' instead of intoning the correct mantra 'The absence of evidence is always evidence of absence but not proof of absence'.
10. Insist the archaeology is there but has not been found yet. More research grants will be needed. Possibly ad infinitum if (9) is correct.

The merits or otherwise of these arguments can be judged by examining the archaeological backdrop to the *Hereford Gospels*. The wider picture is unpromising

> The archaeological evidence for Anglo-Saxon Herefordshire is disappointingly sparse. Much of our evidence comes from chance finds, with Hereford itself being the only major area of archaeological importance for this period. This lack of evidence supports the

description of this period – in Herefordshire at least –
as the "Dark Ages"

So it will have to be the town of Hereford itself

> Hereford is very important as a Saxon town –
> archaeological interpretation has been used across the
> archaeological world. If the interpretation of Hereford
> changes, it has national implications

They don't half give hostages to fortune. We had better pick up the
gauntlet. Speaking of which, what kind of defensive arrangements
did Hereford go in for? It is after all, literally, the 'ford of the heere',
heere being Anglo-Saxon for army. Since we have been assured that 'as
goes Hereford so goes the nation', we might first consider the general
defensive arrangements made by Anglo-Saxons during the period AD
500 – 900. These must have been extensive and nation-wide because

a) the Anglo-Saxons had just arrived from Germany (or
   wherever) and were in the process of ousting the native
   Britons. They did this with such brutishness that in an
   astonishingly short period of time millions of exclusively
   British-speaking Britons were apparently replaced by
   millions of exclusively English-speaking Anglo-Saxons
b) this process was simultaneously being mirrored by
   competing brutes like the Picts, the Irish and the Welsh.

Extensive, yes. Found by archaeologists, not yet.

> One of the problems of Anglo-Saxon archaeology is
> the identification of 8th century royal strongholds ...
> Hereford, situated on a border which was not stabilized
> until the Norman Conquest, would appear to be one
> of the most promising places to look for these elusive
> earthworks

which continue to be elusive, before, during and after the eighth century.
The very early days of Hereford are definitely in the not-yet category

> The earliest finds are presumed to be Roman but
> no definitive dating seems to have been done: a few
> undated ditches, pits and post-holes of probable
> Roman or pre-late Saxon date

All the familiar techniques are on display. Note the casual 'either-or', Roman or not-Roman. If archaeologists can't tell the difference between Glorious Classical and Direst Dark Age, we're all in trouble. This is carefully ignored by the insertion, in this one sentence, of no less than five suitably deprecatory qualifiers: *presumed, no definitive, seems, a few, probably.* But the real corker is the invention of an entire and hitherto unsuspected period of history, the *pre-late Saxon.* Let us discover when that was

> **A north-south ditch ran through the western part of the site, containing animal bone and Roman tile. This was later filled with disarticulated human bone (5000+ individuals), most likely disturbed during construction of the Norman Cathedral**

A thousand years of history swept up in a single paragraph. Either this is Anglo-Saxons dying in the last ditch to defend their beloved town or it is local landfill. It cannot be the latter because Christians do not do that sort of thing with fellow-Christians and would imply there was no Christianity in Hereford between Roman times and Norman times. Which would never do.

To identify the next stage in the hunt for the elusive earthworks, it will be necessary to employ the 'apparently' dodge in its 'appears' and 'perhaps' guises. In which case, better start with a 'certainly'

> **It certainly appears that there was a settlement in Hereford from around 700, when the kingdoms of the Magonsaete and Mercia were amalgamated. It was perhaps at this time that an earthen bank and ditch was constructed to contain the city**

It's a start.

> **An eroded bank with a partially silted-up ditch on its western side, crossed the site in a north-south direction to the west of the period 2 building. No dating material was found but the feature was stratigraphically later than the destruction of the period 1 grain dryers and earlier than the period 4 rampart**

Ah, a rampart. That's more like it

> The bank and ditch, which were seen on other sites to
> the postholes in the tail of the rampart indicate that
> there was a strong timber construction to prevent
> collapse at the rear, and this may have been tied with a
> timber platform to the timber face (seen at Cantilupe
> Street), thus entirely boxing in the rampart. There
> was no evidence to date the construction of this
> rampart, the radiocarbon dates from the timbers being
> questionable

Radiocarbon dates are often 'questionable' though the preferred term now is 'inconclusive'. Did the wooden rampart do its job?

> In the 8th and 9th centuries Hereford and its
> surrounding area were attacked by the Welsh, and the
> earthen rampart was replaced by a stone and gravel
> rampart

Much better. Stone and gravel can't be radiocarbon-dated.

> A lightly mortared stone wall (wall 2), partly built of
> re-used Roman masonry including quern fragments,
> was situated on the rear part of the period 5a rampart
> crest.

We are not told how old the mortar was but 'lightly' suggests it would indeed need some buttressing from five hundred year old Roman masonry. You just can't get the materials nowadays. Querns fill gaps in any age.

> A metalled path, some 3m wide, cut into the tail of the
> rampart, was probably constructed during period 5b, and
> a gully, further to the east, probably acted as a drainage
> or as a property boundary

Sounds more like keeping the neighbours out to me but I don't know what it's like having Anglo-Saxons for neighbours. Well, I suppose I do, I'm officially one myself but you know what I mean. Did it keep the Welsh out? Here are two more variants on 'apparently', see if you can spot them

> A considerable time elapsed between the building of
> a permanent defensive work around the city and the
> re-building of it as a more substantial city wall. This

re-building is most likely to have occurred around 913-915, when Hereford was attacked by the Vikings

A 'considerable' time indeed though I should have thought 'most likely' *before* the ubiquitous Vikings showed up. Or perhaps not! The archaeologists report the Herefordians were reduced to improvising some very make-shift defences

> Even so, the indicated positioning of the breastwork, some 2m behind the defensive face, would have enabled attackers to hide with impunity close to the face of the wall. Under these circumstances, towers constructed as an integral part of the wall or timber platforms projecting over the top of the wall would have been a logical and necessary part of the defensive work and may provide an explanation for the apparent breaks in the face of the wall ... The wall could not have stood to any great height and was dependent on the turf and clay rampart for its defensive strength

No wonder the Anglo-Saxons put up such a feeble show when the Normans arrived. *They* weren't standing for any nonsense

> The front parts of the periods 5 and 6 defensive features were completely removed and replaced by the 13th century medieval wall

All in all, so far as Hereford's defences go, archaeologists have not covered themselves in glory. Historians have not felt inclined to help them out

> None of the several contemporary accounts of the disturbances in Hereford in AD 1139 give any indication that the city had town walls ... the Charter of AD 1189, which allowed the citizens to farm the rent of their town, provided they helped to enclose it, is the first documentary reference to a renewed interest in the city's defences

To sum up local military infrastructure: (1) Hereford is on the Anglo-Welsh border so the Normans built a wall (2) some time after walls ceased to be militarily operative, the town became the headquarters of the SAS.

But that is military, this book is concerned with things ecclesiastical and there should be plenty of ecclesiastical archaeology because Herefordian Christianity goes back a ways

> **Hereford has been the centre of a diocese since the late 7th century and there are also traditions of an earlier Celtic church here**

Traditions cannot be dug up, best stick to the Anglo-Saxon period

> **Cuthbert, Bishop of Hereford from 736-740 (and afterwards Archbishop of Canterbury) set up a cross to commemorate Milfrith, king of the Magonsaete, and three earlier bishops**

Oh goody, an actual cross with actual inscriptions

> **He is credited with the composition of an epitaph for the tomb of his three predecessors at Hereford. The cathedral church of the see may not even have been located at Hereford in Cuthbert's time**

A crying shame but little old Hereford could still edge into the Guinness Book of Records

> **This dedication suggests that Milfrith, grandson of the last Mercian king, Penda, had founded a cathedral city in Hereford prior to this date, which would make it one of the earliest cathedral cities in Western Europe**

A tricky one for the Guinness editors, could one or the other of the national agencies assist?

> **The remains of a Saxon child estimated to have been between the ages of ten and 12 at the time of death were unearthed at Hereford Cathedral as part of an excavation funded by the Heritage Lottery**

But for some reason the cathedral did not prove a popular choice for burial on the part of the citizenry at large

> **The body was buried under the Saxon palace, two hundred years earlier than any other burial in the close**

They might not know where the bodies are buried but at least they now had a palace to go along with the cathedral

> **At the time of the burial, a Saxon palace is thought to have stood on the site. "We are still investigating it."**

Investigating what, pray? A palace or a cathedral? Both!

> **The project revealed a possible Saxon palace built near the cathedral between 850 and 950 AD**

I thought we hadn't found the cathedral. Oh well, never mind, that's just the situation in Hereford – obviously Anglo-Saxon Christian Herefordshire would need plenty of ordinary churches for ordinary people and we know there were *lots* because the Normans did not just rebuild them in stone

> **Many of the churches in Herefordshire that were once dedicated to Saxon saints were re-dedicated to Norman saints**

Norman saints ... a curious concept. Christian saints are supposed to be for all the ages and for all the people but one must, I suppose, allow a certain amount of latitude in these matters. The parishioners clearly soon forgot their old favourites and took these foreign sub-deities to their hearts. They damn well better if England is not to join Wales and Ireland under the cloud of having no Christianity whatsoever before the Normans arrived. In any case these Anglo-Saxon country folk can hardly complain because, after all, they had replaced the Ancient Brits who back in the Roman Empire had had their own saints. Welsh saints? Roman saints? I expect the pope's got a list. Me, I'm not taking sides, I was brought up a Methodist, I don't think we're even allowed saints. But I'd have to check.

Chapter 8

The True History of the World

There are only two significant events in world history: when it started and when it went exponential. The rest is filler. The two events are independent and separated by several thousand years, but both are causally linked to manuscripts. It is universally accepted, even by me, that manuscripts were central to Event One. For those of you unused to the demands of academic departmentalisation

> History (ἱστορία, *historia*) is the study of the past as it is described in written documents

Before 'written documents' everything is *pre*-historic and the domain, not of historians, but of archaeologists. History then necessarily begins with the invention of writing which occurred, as far as we can tell, in Sumer, Mesopotamia, around 3000 BC. Writing produces, or is produced by, a raft of other things, notably cities – *cives* in Latin, hence *civilisation*. The History of the World is faute de mieux the History of Civilisation. Perhaps it ought not to be but there it is. One has to work with the tools one has.

Alongside them anyway. Historians agree with me about Event One, they do not agree with me about Event Two. No academic, no educated person, would accept the *possibility* of an Event Two so entrenched is the assumption that history has been more or less onwards and upwards from 3000 BC to 2000 AD. The most anyone would concede about these five thousand years is there has been the occasional blip along the way and, yes, maybe an uptick towards the end but even the uptick is just the culmination of all that went before. This is completely, totally, muddle-headedly wrong.

Ever wondered why, say, a citizen of Sumer c 3000 BC, setting their DeLorean to three thousand years into the future and landing in Augustan Rome, would find nothing particularly unfamiliar there? 'Same old, same old,' he might complain, 'they haven't even got any Hanging Gardens.' (He stopped off at Babylon along the way.) Ever wondered why our Sumerian, setting the dials to four thousand years into the future and with a wider brief, would discover civilisation *still* had not reached Scandinavia or sub-Saharan Africa? 'Civilisation sure doesn't seem to travel well,' he might opine. Historians do not ask these kinds of questions, they abhor big picture stuff – journalism, they sniff, or worse. Technically they have a point: there is no contemporary written material attesting to any of it. So here's some contemporary written material attesting to it

1. One of the keys to human development is the triple-T, Terrestrial Transport Technology, the best way of moving people, things and information from place to place
2. Without a decent TTT people, things and information tend to stay pretty much where they are
3. At the birth of civilisation in 3000 BC the TTT was the horse and cart (and its variants)
4. After five thousand years of civilisation the TTT was the horse and cart (and its variants)
5. In a hundred and forty-four years, 1825–1969, the TTT went from horse and cart to moon rockets.

Yes, I know all the caveats, thanks. As I say, we're talking Big Picture. Suck it and see. You can always spit it out before the convulsions begin.

*   *   *

Since civilisation seems to have something to do with writing let us begin on firm ground with a couple of obvious truths

1. You speak a language
2. You can write that language down

Now let us begin again by pointing out both statements are not only untrue, they are in the wrong order

1. You can write down a 'word-formulation'
2. You can speak that 'word-formulation'

What you cannot do is

1. Speak a *language* because no such thing has existed where you live for many, many years before you were born

132

2. Write down a *language* because languages cannot be written down.

Languages cannot be written down because they consist of, for practical purposes, an infinite number of sounds. Not just a sound for each word, but because each word can be variously pronounced in different situations, each individual developing his or her own rules about how to do this and the whole thing changes with each succeeding generation. Even if your writing system could somehow encompass all this (a tape recorder does) there would be little point because the people in the next valley over would be speaking a whole different set of sounds.

This situation arises because, before civilisation, human beings' chief diversion was talk and they had had tens of thousands, maybe hundreds of thousands, maybe millions of years to make every dialogue a drama as well as a simple tool of communication. Conversation was conducted in a free-flowing form that defied all rules save those of basic comprehensibility to whomsoever one was speaking to. One wouldn't use that sentence for a start. 'Natural languages' are chaotic universes. English for instance was one once, not now.

Were you minded to keep a permanent record of the natural Sumerian language of c 3000 BC you would either have to invent the tape recorder or a 'word-formulation'. I am sorry to use such a clunky expression as *word-formulation* but historians, archaeologists, linguists, philologists and anthropologists do not accept any of the above, so no word has ever been coined for a 'natural language'. For them, language is language because it is the way *we* do it – we write as we speak. It does not occur to them that what we speak is a *word-formulation* which we call a *language* but is in reality a limited palette of sounds mapping phonetically to an alphabet of a few dozen sound-symbols. They apply their speak-as-you-write rule rigidly which means whenever they come across writing they assume what is on the page is the spoken language of the writers.

On hearing all this your first reaction will be to suppose I am drawing a distinction that is both petty and arbitrary. Your brain always converts unsettling concepts into something familiar so, if you are an English-speaker, you will probably be thinking in terms of

1) Dialect English and
2) Standard English

Tell your brain to pipe down, this is *not* what I am saying. Neither Standard English nor any of its regional variations are 'natural languages', they are all 'word-formulations'. When a London music hall comedian c 1900 AD performs at the Glasgow Alhambra everyone concerned is speaking Standard English, only the accents are different. It is true both performer and audience have retained a few consciously antique language markers for local bonding purposes but they are all speaking Standard English.

If a London philologist had visited the Glasgow of 1300 AD he would have found he and they were speaking mutually incomprehensible languages though if the philologist listened carefully he would recognise they were both speaking closely related languages – even, depending on the way these things are classified, the same language. The philologist would not have been able to record in writing the Glaswegian one and only with the greatest difficulty his own. He was already, by 1300, *nearly* speaking a word-formulation, originally the London/South Midland version of natural English but thereafter it gradually became a proper word-formulation which his philological successors would label variously as post-vowel shift English, Standard English, literary English, RP English, Queen's English, BBC English.

The c 1300 Glaswegians were also *nearly* speaking and writing their own word-formulation though they understandably labelled it 'Scots'. *Lallan* [lowland] Scots to distinguish it, not from *Inglis* with which they had minimal contact, but from highland Scots *Gaelic* with which they had all too maximal contact. It is a wonder the lowland Scots, speaking a 'language' cognate with their southern English neighbours, elected (if that's the right word) to form a country with their northern neighbours, the wholly alien Gaelic-speakers. But later on they elected (nearly the right word) to join the English after all whereupon Lallan Scots died out and Standard English ruled. By the by, Scottish historians, ever the lackeys of English historians, are perfectly content to accept the theory they acquired their language from a handful of Anglo-Saxons who occupied the south-eastern corner of their country for a few years. They differ from English historians as to how this was done. In England, apparently, the Anglo-Saxons either killed off the natives or drove them into Wales; in Scotland the Anglo-Saxons somehow 'persuaded' everyone to start speaking Anglo-Saxon without further ado. As I say,

134

the Scots always defer to the English. Or they may wish to defer to me instead and send the whole theory packing by adopting the common-sense position that Anglo-Saxon has nothing whatsoever to do with either *Inglis* or *Scots* which were the languages everybody was speaking when the Anglo-Saxons arrived. It is difficult to predict which theory would appeal more to the Scots. They may wish to hold a referendum.

I appreciate all this may be difficult to get your English-speaking head around so try this experiment: go to Rome (today's Rome, not Roman Empire Rome) and try ordering a cup of coffee in Latin. When that fails, ask the waiter (preferably in Italian) where his language comes from. He (their gender enlightenment is Roman Empire Roman) will tell you (proudly, if he is an Italian Roman) it derives from Latin. Ask him what Romans were speaking before Latin and he will ask you if you want a panini with your coffee. (Or would he say 'panino', I must find out.)

He won't have a clue because linguists don't have a clue. Linguists are a clueless lot. It requires no more than a basic understanding of peoples' attachment to their mother tongue to guess that Romans were speaking 'Italian' before there was a Rome though not an 'Italian' much resembling modern Italian. *Standard* Italian is a phonetic word-formulation mapping closely to the twenty-one sounds represented in the Italian alphabet, whereas *Ancient* Italian had the infinite sounds of a natural language. The ancient Italian spoken around Rome would be the *Latsian* variety because the people of the Lazio region of central Italy would be speaking a version all but incomprehensible to their contemporaries in Umbria, Tuscany, Abruzzo and Campania. Just to confuse things further Lazio itself would be something of a linguistic melting pot. A Roman Latsian male would find it difficult to sweet talk a Sabine Latsian female. Next valley over.

This unsatisfactory situation led to some Romans of the fifth/sixth century BC embarking on a radical departure. For Latsians anyway – their northern neighbours, the Etruscans, and their southern neighbours, the Greeks, had already done it. Rome, they decided, needed its own written language, just as the Greeks, the Etruscans and all the successful 'civilisations' around the Mediterranean basin had *their* own written language. They would need their very own 'word-formulation' if Latsian was to be written down. What did they have to do to come up with *Latin*? We don't know from the historical record but we can approximately know by using the few sources we do have, plus common sense, to produce a step-by-step guide:

1. They first had to confront the problem all the others had confronted before them – how to reduce the infinite sounds of Latsian to a manageable number that could be represented by written symbols.
2. This was especially difficult for the Romans because they knew nothing of writing systems that allowed a large number of sounds to be represented on the page – ideograms, pictographs, logographs, syllabaries, graphemes.
3. The only method they *were* familiar with was the phonetic 'alphabet' writing-system invented, as far as we know, by the Phoenicians (the clue is in the name).
4. But which alphabet? Taking someone else's off the shelf would militate against local pride which was the whole point of the exercise.
5. But something completely novel would militate against persuading already literate Latsians, of which there were a great number, to adopt it.
6. So they did what everybody else before them had done (save possibly the Phoenicians): choose an existing alphabet and tweak it enough to make it distinctive.
7. But which alphabet? Phonologically Greek was closest – the Etruscans and the Phoenicians spoke very strange languages.
8. So Greek it was, plus tweaks.
9. How now, brown cow, does one set about fitting the infinite sounds of the natural Latsian language into the straitjacket of the twenty-plus vowels and consonants of a tweaked Greek alphabet?
10. Well, Yulius Cæsar, one can always expand any alphabet by using two-way letter pronunciations and diphthongs.
11. Since infinite still won't go into twenty-something no matter what tricks of the trade are employed, it was quite impractical to write down anything recognisable to a Latsian.
12. The Romans knew what demotic Greek-speaking Greeks had done which was to invent Classical Greek in order to

write down demotic Greek.

13. So they invented *Latin* to write down demotic Latsian.

What were our own dear academics to make of all this thousands of years later? Since academics speak as they write, they assume the ancients spoke as they wrote. Sometimes this is actually true. Cicero spoke as he wrote. But mostly not. Even in Rome. Either way, Roman history can cope. But what happens when literate people occupy the lands of non-literate people and all local written records will of necessity be in the language of the invaders, not in the language of the natives? How does historians' 'speak as they write' rule work when really widespread occupiers of non-literate lands like the Romans are around? It produces some very weird history

1. Whenever the Romans occupy a literate country – say, Greece or Egypt – and therefore the documentation is written in, say, Greek or Egyptian, historians assume the locals carried right on speaking whatever it was they were speaking when the Romans arrived

2. Whenever the Romans occupy a non-literate country – say, France or Spain – and therefore the documentation can only be in Latin, historians assume the locals must have ditched their language and gone over en masse to speaking Latin

3. In such cases the locals set about evolving Latin into a 'Romance language' e.g. French and Spanish [Romance = from Roman i.e. Latin]

4. If the locals do not speak a Romance language – say, Basque or Dutch – this cannot have been the case so an exception to the rule is applied: they were hold-outs who did not take up Latin for some unspecified reason

5. Should a specified reason subsequently become available, the rule can be re-applied e.g. Brittany is occupied by Welsh-speakers and the Bretons switch over en masse to Welsh; Britain is occupied by Anglo-Saxons and the Britons switch over en masse to English etc etc

6. Once these 'literary occupations' have taken place, everyone lives happily ever after language-wise. Any subsequent

foreign-speaking invaders occupying areas of Europe for just as long as the Romans did – say, Goths, Arabs, Franks – will not be able to perform the old language switcheroo.

✷   ✷   ✷

To set the record straight all that is required is to do what no historian can ever do, ignore the historical record. Since we have extensive *modern* records for how all this is done in the present day we can apply the known known to the known unknown. The 'knowns' in this case being the languages of Esperanto and Hebrew. This is what we *know*

1. how easy it is to *create* artificial languages. The Esperantists had no difficulty coming up with a complete vocabulary, grammar and syntax
2. how easy it is to *write* an artificial language. Esperanto was entirely phonetic and mapped to a tweaked but familiar alphabet
3. how easy it is to *speak* an artificial language. Anything that could be written in phonetic Esperanto could by definition be spoken in Esperanto
4. how difficult it is to *persuade* anyone to do (2) or (3) unless there is a pressing reason why they should
5. if there is a pressing reason why they should, e.g. polyglot immigrants arriving in the new state of Israel, they might be persuaded
6. if for *political* reasons it was decided the common language should not be any of the ones the immigrants already spoke and wrote, e.g. Yiddish, German, English, Polish, Russian, Arabic, but an artificial one, e.g. Hebrew, that none of them spoke or wrote (except maybe a bit from *shul*) then
7. it was a piece of cake.

We can apply these known general principles to see how the Latsian-speaking Romans were faring in the sixth century BC. First the bad news

1. Like the Esperantists, the Romans had no trouble coming up with Latin but found few Romans wanted to ditch the

138

wonderfully expressive Latsian they had painstakingly learned at their mother's knee in order to do it all over again for the stilted rigidities of Latin

2. Unless maybe they wanted to be literate except, the Latinists were disconcerted to find, any Roman who wanted to be literate was already literate in Greek or Etruscan

3. There was nobody to write to in Latin. Why learn Latin to write to other Romans when you could pop round and speak to them in person in Latsian? If you really wanted to write to them they must already be literate in Greek or Etruscan, as presumably were you. And of course there was no point in writing Latin to non-Latsians

4. There was nothing worth *reading* in Latin whereas Greek (we don't know about Etruscan) was famously awash with all the great classics of literature.

Now the good news

1. Romans who were literate in Greek or Etruscan were already marked out from Romans who were illiterate; now Romans literate *in Latin* were marked out from merely literate Romans

2. Latinists could communicate with other Latinists irrespective of anyone's mother tongue. Speaking Latsian was irrelevant

3. By the second generation, Latin did not need to be 'learned' since these marked-out Latinists tended to marry one another and brought up their children to speak Latin. You were born to the purple

4. You stayed in the purple no matter how many of the hoi polloi *learned* Latin because, as people speaking a second language, they betrayed that fact every time they spoke Latin. Them and us cannot be counterfeited

5. People in the purple tend to be the people in power and hence can promote policies favouring Latin-speakers – in particular mother's knee Latin-speakers – for a vast array of state purposes, especially those that tended to keep the people in power in power

6. An oligarchical state with internal cohesiveness and expansionary potential had been produced with remarkable speed and efficiency
7. How *much* expansionary potential would be determined by competition with Greeks, Etruscans, Carthaginians, Egyptians etc who had already adopted the same model
8. History will decide
9. Ensure all historians are brought up in a tradition which is skewed wildly towards Latin (and to be on the safe side, Greek) sources
10. History has decided that...

All this applies functionally, if not in detail, to all civilisations from Sumer onwards. We know all civilisations from Sumer onwards failed to achieve exponential lift-off, except our own. It is not unreasonable then to apply a bit of hypothetical correlation, All of Them vs Us, and since literacy in a demotic language is one difference between Them and Us, we might tentatively propose this was a critical factor. Even the critical factor.

In terms of *any* development the Chinese did by far the best but they could not, it seemed, get over the artificial literary language hurdle so long as they were speaking Han and writing Mandarin. The Chinese certainly had the option of mass literacy – all (Han) Chinese today speak Han and write Mandarin so it is certainly technically possible, but presumably the Mandarinate did not permit such liberties. However, generally, the 'artificial literacy barrier' does not appear to be *political* since each civilisation had its own variant form of literacy and its own variant form of how literacy was diffused through its population. Nonetheless, all of them ended up *functionally* as citizen/helot societies, a literate minority and an illiterate majority. It would appear that literacy itself was creating the barrier to development and the only common factor in all ancient literacy models was that the language spoken by the helots was not the language spoken by the citizens.

All ancient civilisations were good at some things, not so good at others. That is not surprising. What is surprising is they were always the *same* things

Good: monumental building, roads, armies, state religions
Fair: metallurgy for military and artistic purposes, observational astronomy, basic geometry, public art, rhetorical literature
Woeful: technology

Everything in the first category was pre-figured in pre-history; everything in the second category serves in the attainment of the first category; the third category provides lift-off. That is why our time-travelling Sumerian would find nothing strange about Augustan Rome. He might admire the aqueducts but that is because Rome needs to employ monumental building to get a decent water supply whereas a river civilisation like Babylon could afford to apply its monumental building talents to hanging gardens. Neither place got much beyond the simple Archimedean screw when it came to hydrological technology. They did not, for instance, need sophisticated pumping technology to, for instance, mine everything they required so they never developed, for instance, pumping technology for deeper mines using, for instance, steam engines thereby, for instance, triggering Industrial Revolutions. Steam engines do not require modern metallurgy – any ancient smith could have knocked one up – if only they had been engineers as well as smiths. But for some reason a few basic technological principles were forever out of reach so long as 'knowledge' was the purview of mandarinates, priesthoods, academies, schools of rhetoric, monastery scriptoria and universities. Ancient civilisations could produce all kinds of wonders but not engineers.

* * *

The history of the engineer starts with realtor-monks of eleventh century England, or so I like to think though in truth it might have been elsewhere in Western Europe. They needed to write into their land charters the names of people and places that were presenting them with a novel problem. Their familiar Latin was an exemplary medium for recording *Marcus Apenninus of Eboracum*, it could cope well enough with *Gudrum Bloodaxe of York*, it was not suited at all to *Enid Witherall of Hoe Street, Walthamstow* and unfortunately, by the eleventh century, land belonged more often to the Enids than to the Marcuses and the

141

Gudrums. The technique for rendering names and places had been to take the demotic name and render it into Latin by *transliteration* using certain rules arbitrarily applied. Words like *Enid, Witherall, Hoe* and *Walthamstow* could happily be given this treatment to produce a Latin equivalent for each word but, unlike Marcus Apenninus and Gudrum Bloodaxe, Enid Witherall was not known by name to any scribe other than the transliterator so *his* arbitrary transliteration would not necessarily be *their* transliteration. Mrs Witherall's identity might easily be challenged and as her estate was quite valuable this could prove awkward.

Feudal Europe was based on individual land ownership so a solution had to be found. Necessity/mother/invention meant a solution was found. Instead of transliterating they could use the phonetic letters of their alphabet to write approximately the sounds of the demotic words Enid, Witherall, Hoe and Walthamstow. It was still arbitrary because demotic English in the eleventh century consisted mainly of sounds that could not be captured exactly by the Latin alphabet but the realtors found to their surprise this did not matter! So long as you *spoke* eleventh century demotic English, you could guess with almost complete fidelity who the Latin letters in *Enid, Witherall, Hoe* and *Walthamstow* referred to. It helped if a new letter, W, was added to the Latin alphabet in order to capture that particularly English aspirate at the start of *Witherall* and *Walthamstow* to distinguish it from the Latin aspirate of *Hoe* and the non-aspirate of *Enid*. What's more, this new letter which, at the start of a word meant an aspirate, could be put unambiguously at the end of a word to get that awful meow sound at the end of *Walthamstow*. Now they were motoring.

But not terribly fast and not terribly far. These realtor-monks, being professional scribes, could laboriously apply these new rules for spelling out discrete words like *Enid, Witherall, Hoe,* and *Walthamstow* for other realtor-monks (or canon lawyers) to read back equally laboriously. It was no use for *text* because writing and reading continuous English of any length was even more laborious. One thousand AD demotic English was a natural language and would-be literate people in it would have to make up and carry around a vast number of conventions to get it all down on paper, even approximately. And even if they managed that, folks fifty miles away, speaking a different variant of one thousand AD demotic English, would need a whole different set of conventions. To be honest, when it came to text, Latin did the job much better in every way. Once the innovation had bedded down, it was found the monks of Old England had made no advance in human civilisation beyond some improvements in land registration practices. A seed, however, had been sown. An essential seed if the English monks' English-speaking descendants were ever to get to the moon. **The first brick in the wall of exponential development had been laid.**

*   *   *

Anyone thinking the New History of the World is getting a wee bit Anglo-centric will be relieved to hear it was the French who took the next step. To follow the story it is essential to appreciate there was nothing special about Western Europe. Yes, it had had experience of superior civilisations – Phoenician, Greek, Carthaginian, Roman, Umayyad – but in the period AD 1000–1500 it was and remained behind the Chinese, the Indians, the Persians and the Ottomans in overall development. If anything it had gone *backwards*. A citizen of Augustan Rome would have been disgusted by the Rome of the Borgias. Never mind hanging gardens, never mind aqueducts, they scarcely had drinking fountains. And the arts! My dear, one shudders. But it is the military sphere – always the touchstone of contemporary technology – that best sums up the state of Western Europe at this time. Any average Greek hoplite army would have made mincemeat of the English at Agincourt

> Look out, lads, incoming! Arrows. Now there's something you don't see every week. Non-compound longbows judging by the trajectory. Nice grouping. Demonstrates adequate training. Make a note of that, adjutant. Eyes right, everyone, here comes the cavalry. What are those things? Oh, stirrups. Whatever will they think of next. I wonder if horses charge formed bodies of infantry knowing they've got stirrups on. Apparently not. Good grief, who's this lot? Men-at-arms in fully-articulated plate armour? Bet that costs a drachma or two. No wonder there's so few of them. All the same,

odd thing to bring onto a battlefield. Front two ranks, push-of-pike, on my command. They'll fall over after a few backward steps. Try not to damage the armour – that's good stuff, you can see that from here. Stop smirking the rest of you, you're not in the Theban army now.

And yet shortly it would all be different and the Western Europeans would conquer the world. How did they manage this, armed only with nascent written demotics? There were formidable obstacles to overcome before the Age of Artificial Elite Literary Word-Formulations could be brought to an end. For instance

1. The old system held all the levers of power, including the power to determine who could read and write, what they could read and write, and in what language they could read and write.
2. Even if a written demotic became widely available there was no reason for the general public to learn it because there was nothing of any interest to read in it.
3. Even if there was something of interest to read, the medium of reading – manuscripts – was too expensive for anyone to bother. Name any book you would pay £500 to read.

Getting past (1) and (2) was difficult for the Europeans because the Church held both de facto and de jure powers, which meant written material consisted of the Bible, saints' lives, ecclesiastical land charters and state papers, all in Latin except for some demotic sprinkling. To move things along would require people who, as an absolute minimum

a) took no notice of the Church
b) were familiar with literary languages other than Latin
c) were neither monks nor bureaucrats
d) had a professional need to write things down in the demotic
e) had access to people who could pay for their professional services
f) and powerful enough to protect them from the ire of the Church

Got it in one! The troubadours of Septimania. This is the area of southern France most of us would call either Provence or the Languedoc but people from those parts with an elevated political consciousness might call it Occitania because the local language is – increasingly *was* – Occitan, intermediate between French and Catalan. This was not what made Septimania special in 1000 AD, that was Septimania's enthusiasm for syncretic religions drawn from Muslim, Jewish, Arian and Bogomil sources – anything so long as it wasn't Roman Christianity. Why this was is not clear, nothing is clear about Western Europe *c* 1000 AD, but it probably had something to do with Septimania being awash with literary languages other than Latin – Arabic, Hebrew and Greek to name three. So who were the troubadours and what was their part in the unleashment of Europe?

Thus far in human history, the performing arts had always been labouring under a severe handicap. Should you wish to be a respectable theatre actor you had to

a) learn your lines
b) learn to read in order to learn your lines
c) learn a foreign language because the lines were written in a language you did not speak
d) learn how to give a dramatic performance in a foreign language
e) learn to give a dramatic performance in a foreign language that was horribly inexpressive because it was designed to be written by traders, bureaucrats, priests and academics
f) learn how to perform to traders, bureaucrats, priests and academics if you wanted an audience who could understand a single word you were saying

Nevertheless, judging by the size and number of ancient amphitheatres, there was no shortage either of performers or audiences. Thousands came whether they understood the words or not. This is not unprecedented, millions of people today attend operas performed in languages neither they nor the singers can speak. It did though mean the repertoire was limited to staple themes, simplistic plots, fanciful settings, formulaic productions and over-stylised performances. Classical theatre was much the same.

Over in the less favoured parts of town, there was *demotic* theatre. Though not necessarily *in* a theatre. Euripides is fine for special occasions but what we really want for a good night out is something we can relate to and most of us don't go round killing our parents. Ancient demotic theatre though had problems of its own. Since it was by definition non-literate there could be no lines to be learned. Actors had to be verbally taught lines by rote or by freely extemporising from familiar material and, while it was certainly easier to do this in their own expressive, endlessly variable natural language to audiences who shared that language, demotic theatre had strict limitations

   a) it didn't travel well – fifty miles away the language variations were too great
   b) the audience couldn't pay much – the nobs either did not speak the local demotic or wouldn't be seen dead
   c) there could be no specialisation of labour – the performers were necessarily the playwrights
   d) the repertoire was limited to what could be easily memorised or extemporised
   e) the audiences actually preferred endlessly repeated (with a bit of extemporising) versions of time-honoured themes – mainly illicit sex or, if that wasn't allowed, licit religion.

So much for educated people and the broad masses, so much for classical theatre and demotic theatre. But there was *another* audience who *could* pay and were on the lookout for something a bit more ambitious. The ruling elite. The court. The people Shakespeare had watching Pyramus and Thisbe from the sidelines. Now top people are not great fans of Euripides. Or opera, for that matter. Some are, most aren't, and they could afford troupes to perform material more to their taste. Except before 1000 AD there wasn't any material to their taste. Performing troupes were constrained by the same technical considerations as above. In fact *both* sets of constraints because with the Roman Empire long gone nobody in the ruling elite spoke either Latin or Greek, by now strictly scribal languages. The higher-ups spoke demotic languages (though not always the demotic langue du pays).

Historians understand all this and conjure up visions of bards reciting genealogies but historians rarely point out bardic recitations grow wearisome after about one hearing – after about two verses to be perfectly honest. Masques and suchlike were impractical on a regular basis and anyway grow wearisome too on a regular basis. What to do? Well, some Septimanian troubadours thought, let's get these monkish scribes who have learned how to transcribe demotic languages to teach us how to do it. Learning to read and write in the vernacular took time and trouble but paid spectacular dividends if you were in the bards-to-nobs business because

1) it did not matter that Occitan written in Latin letters was laborious to decipher, they were learning lines for business not reading for pleasure
2. it did not matter that the Occitan of Marseilles was wildly different from the Occitan of Perpignan, both were approximations of literary Occitan
3. specialisation of labour was now achievable because there was no need for the people writing the material to perform it
4. this material, being *de novo*, could be tailored to the contemporary tastes of court folk. Out with Theseus and Ariadne, in with Tristan and Isolde
5. the repertoire was constantly expanding since writing plays was a paying proposition for the first time since Euripides
6. especially when the repertoire went international – Occitanian material (and methods) could be translated into any other demotic written language
7. of which predictably there were soon quite a number in other parts of western Europe

We know something along these lines happened from the historical record but we also know from the same historical record it made little difference to the overall development of Western Europe. Courtly establishments are not great ones for societal innovation. But they are highly enthusiastic about artistic innovation so the new written demotics were here to stay and the clamant objections of the mandarinate in the Church, the monasteries, the law courts and the universities, determined to keep their Latin monopoly, were firmly resisted. The spread of literary vernaculars was unstoppable. **The second brick in the wall of exponential development had been laid.**

*   *   *

There was still the same old problem. Why would anyone bother to learn to read and write unless there was a professional need to do so? Sure, there was at last a literature in your own language but would you pay five hundred pounds for a *Piers Ploughman,* a *Canterbury Tales,* a *Gawain and the Green Knight*? Nor me. But I might like to *listen* to Piers Ploughman, the Canterbury Tales and Gawain and the Green Knight and that would be no great pleasure were I speaking an English variant different to the one(s) spoken by the writers of Piers Ploughman, the Canterbury Tales or Gawain and the Green Knight. In fact it would be most unlikely Piers Ploughman, the Canterbury Tales or Gawain and the Green Knight would be written at all were there not a pre-existing class of Standard English-speakers to read them and to listen to them. By the fourteen hundreds there was such a class because once demotic literacy is introduced there is a constant push-pull towards standardisation of the spoken form around the written form, though it had little to do with any penchant for poetry.

The literate class is no different from any other elite grouping, they like to signal their eliteness to one other, and especially to the non-elite. There is little point being part of an elite if this basic minimum cannot be met. One does not park one's yacht over the horizon. It's bad enough having to live on the damned thing. A demotic–literate society presented a brand new elite-signalling problem. Hitherto in world history, speaking *the elite language* separated upper from lower. In Roman Britain, for instance, there had been Latin-speakers, there had been 'British'-speakers, and nary the twain; in medieval England everyone spoke English. There were, it is true, a scribal form of English and natural spoken English(es) but that distinction was of no use for signalling purposes – carrying around a copy of the *Ancrene Wisse* didn't really cut it. Besides, the elite of medieval England were frequently illiterate. Unless you *spoke* Standard English. That would cut it. It was a wretchedly pared down language and there were lots of rules to remember but what did that matter when your eliteness was established every time you opened your mouth and, unlike Latin, you didn't have to learn it. Eliteness is hereditary, you were already fluent by age five.

148

At the end of the Middle Ages this Standard English had already ceased to be a language in the ordinary sense being grammatically formalised around the rules of Latin and having a near-phonetic vocabulary that mapped to the Latin alphabet (plus some introduced English letters, plus a selection of digraphs, plus a morass of weird pronunciation rules). If it is difficult to accept just how radical the shift is from a natural idiomatic regional English to Standard English, consider the astonishing fact there is no second person singular in Standard English. This major inconvenience came about purely from elite signalling. There is no *th* sound in the Latin alphabet so scribes used *Y* to write the *th* sound, which was fine for Ye Olde Englyshe Tea Shoppe but not so fine when anybody who wanted to write *thou,* was obliged to write *you,* and anybody reading *you* when they were actually reading *thou,* ended up saying *you* whether they meant you personally or you collectively. Better to show one was a member of the elite than worry about ambiguity.

English came late to the game and is still quirky even in its Standard form. Over in Italy, where the alphabet had been specifically designed for local use, and where they had been mapping natural Italian (especially natural Florentine) for a lot longer than the English, they had produced a near-phonetic Standard Italian as early as Petrarch's time. Much, I might add, to the detriment of Italian literature. While we were exploiting the quirks of English to become world leaders in every branch of the written word, the Italians were stuck with being world leaders in opera. But in England, in Italy, in most of Western Europe, the spread of *standardised* written demotics meant **the third brick in the wall of exponential development had been laid.**

*   *   *

Still not enough. Manuscripts are expensive and so long as the medium is expensive, the message is expensive. So long as the message is expensive, the message will be limited to the Bible, courtly romances, poems for recitation, plays for performing, translations of the classics, academic treatises, governmental records, mercantile communications. This is a fundamental rule irrespective of the language the message is couched in and no matter how many people are able to read it.

Medieval demotic literature was no better suited for developmental purposes than everything that had gone before. *Before printing*. Cheap printing, moveable-type printing – the Chinese as per usual already had expensive block printing so continued turning out Confucius, courtly romances, poems and the rest.

There is nothing in the least technically difficult about moveable-type printing. It did not need advanced metallurgical skills, woodcraft folk could do it. Anybody could have done it from Sumer onwards so we can only presume it was the churls of Western Europe who did it because they were the only people in the world, the only people thus far in world history, that had a mass market in standardised literary demotics for their products. Memo to the Chinese: alphabets help too. It is difficult coming up with any other explanation because there was nothing special about Europe c 1450. In every other respect, in comparison to most of the civilisations from Sumer onwards, Medieval Europe was depressingly undeveloped, her most obvious contribution to the advance of humankind being the Gothic cathedral and that was just their version of the monumental building bug that had infected everybody else from Sumer onwards. Still and all, with the arrival of printing **the fourth brick in the wall of exponential development had been laid.**

✻   ✻   ✻

Forget the Renaissance. That was just getting back to the start line (the clue is in the name). It was Printing-plus-Reformation that was important. Printing for the cheapness, Reformation for being allowed to exploit the printing. Once there was a Bible in High German at five pounds a throw *and* they were allowed to read it, every German was potentially his own Renaissance Man. This was not the case for Printing-but-no-Reformation: Spaniards, for instance, were mired in the era of Don Quixote, the Green Knight. But Reformations are a mixed blessing. Germans were only *potentially* developmentally-minded book-devouring all-rounders because revolutions have a nasty habit of replacing the old with the new-old. Lutheran and Calvinist regimes turned out to be just as restrictive about what people should be allowed to read as Catholic ones. The Germans did try out various freer forms of Protestantism, but Anabaptists and their fellow schismatic schismatics discovered freeform tends to be dispatched in short order by non-freeform. Thank God.

But it did mean Germany was unavailable for much in the way of developmental advance while they sorted out their religious differences, and it was those sensible Dutch who stole the German bikes. If there was any justice in the world it ought to be the Dutch we have to thank for the modern world but they never quite made the leap. Too busy avoiding being dispatched in short order by Habsburgs and Bourbons. It was left to the English to usher in exponentiality (hooray). This is odd because the English are nothing special (boo). But they soon were

1500 England a bit behind Europe, Europe a bit behind everyone else

1600 England has caught up with Europe, Europe has caught up with everyone else

1700 England a bit ahead of Europe, Europe a bit ahead of everyone else

1800 England out of sight, Europe out of sight

The explanation for these twin trends could *ex hypothesi* go something like this

1. Europe alone in the world has standardised literary demotics
2. Europe alone in the world develops cheap books in standardised demotics
3. Protestant Europe alone in Europe has unrestricted cheap books in standardised demotics
4. England alone in Protestant Europe converts unrestricted cheap books in standardised demotics into an exponential industrial revolution

except (4) seems to lack even a hypothetical justification and if the English are nothing special, that last decisive step cannot be explained by native genius. Though since England did produce a native genius at this time, we might begin with Isaac Newton. My animus against academia tempts me to place the Rise of England to the day Newton left Cambridge to become a stay-at-home genius but this is not a suitable point for exponential departure since

151

i) Newton is a very medieval figure who read and wrote in Latin and was more crackpot mystic than Protestant

ii) Newtonian science, science of any kind, played a negligible part in the Great Leap Forward. Science is always overrated. Science-and-technology are only bracketed together because technologists crave respectability, scientists crave relevance and the rest of us crave the assurance somebody somewhere must know what on earth is going on

iii) being in or out of a university is irrelevant (except in terms of producing originality) because universities are unsuited for human development, personal or collective. They are medieval institutions with entry requirements that preserve them as self-perpetuating oligarchical guilds with a jargon impenetrable to outsiders – formerly Latin, latterly academese. In any case they must have been irrelevant to the medieval/modern interface because everyone had had universities for centuries, not just in England and not just in Europe. Guilds are always inimical to change though, as it happens, universities will soon cease to be guilds because on present and exponential trends everyone will soon be required to attend university, and nobody knows what happens to guilds when all are members. It's never been tried before. Probably not being in a guild will become a badge of distinction. It's too late for me, my children, but think what it would be like if your gap year could last a lifetime.

No, the starting gun must be technological, and it is hard to argue with the invention of the steam engine. Specifically Newcomen's steam engine of 1712. I assume the name 'Newcomen' is coincidental rather than coined but either way he was a very modern phenomenon, an ironmonger and a Baptist. Though not the inventor of the steam engine, just the inventor of the steam engine that took off. There had been plenty of steam engines before, they are not technically difficult to build. Anybody from Sumer onwards could have done it – Hero of Alexandria did do it and doubtless unrecorded others also did it in antiquity. Even in the seventeenth century the French and the Spanish did it before the English but they, like the ancients, lacked Baptist ironmongers.

Engineers not inventors are what is needed to get steam engines off the ground, France and Spain preferred artists to artisans. Baroque is what you get without a Reformation. Baroque factories even! It is not that Catholic Europe did not understand what was required. Louis XIV was desperate to keep up with the go-ahead Dutch but whenever he let the go-ahead Colbert loose with unlimited budgets and unprecedented powers, all France got for her money was more efficient tapestry factories. That is the nature of top-down decision making.

N.B. libertarians. Any country that wants to develop rapidly, and knows how to do it because other countries have already shown how, *should* use top-down decision making. It is much more difficult when nobody knows how, when it is being done for the first time. The insurmountable obstacle being that *all* countries are top-down and any country that is not, will soon cease to be a country. Either the state will dissolve into chaos and/or another state, a top-down state, will take it over. Unless something changed, the world was doomed to an endless diet of top-down regimes and the *top* in top-down never encourage development, being first in the firing line. The trick is not to have anybody at the top *just long enough*. The English achieved this thanks to the English Civil War. But everyone has civil wars, what was so special about theirs?

1) it was discretely regional – most civil wars are messier
2) it was truly Marxian – most civil wars are internecine within the ruling elite
3) it was waged by the populace – most civil wars are oligarchical affairs
4) it was ideological – most civil wars are for simple regime change
5) it was won by the insurgents – most civil wars are won by the incumbents
6) the insurgents voluntarily handed power back to the incumbents. That is unprecedented. Perhaps the English *are* geniuses!

Despite the unceasing claims of historians and political zealots, the English Civil War was a non-event in the general thrust of English history. In religion, zilch. The Elizabethan Settlement of the sixteenth

153

century, consisting of a not very Protestant established Church, mildly restricted properly Protestant churches and a severely restricted Catholic Church, lasted until Catholic Emancipation in the nineteenth century. In politics, zilch. The Civil War was a minor interlude in the leisurely stroll from a strong monarchy and a querulous parliament in the sixteenth century to a strong parliament and a querulous monarchy in the nineteenth century. But the Civil War *was* critical for some radical changes in English literary habits.

For eighteen years, 1642–60, there was mass participatory religious and political theatre. Now this is not so unusual in civil wars either – the same pattern had been witnessed in Florence, Münster, Geneva, Prague and half a hundred other places in Western Europe 1500 – 1700. It was a practice going back to the Roman Republic of the Gracchi, Marius and Caesar; further back to the Greek *polis* and no doubt all the way back to Sumerian city states. But all these évènements were played out by oratory and tumult. That's cities for you. The English Civil War was not just spread over an entire country, it was spread over an entire country with access to cheap printed material in a language by now familiar throughout that entire country. Oratory and tumult might be all the rage in London but in the broad acres everyone was fighting their corner with books and pamphlets.

Before 1642 the English had been no more bookish than anyone else. Thomas More claimed, as far back as the 1520's, half of Londoners were literate but whether this is true in any meaningful sense they sure as hell didn't show it if their reading matter is anything to go by – a thin gruel of religious orthodoxy and highbrow tomes. The only popular works were gruesome martyrologies and almanacs. The Civil War changed all that – suddenly the most astonishing variety of material was required reading. Nobody is interested in politics or religion in good times, everybody is consumed by them in bad times. Where there is demand there shall be supply, unless government and NGO's forbid it. But in times of civil war, government and NGO's are the problem not the solution. For the first time in human history, there was a mass literacy *industry* and no *mandarinate* with the power to keep a lid on things. When the bad times stopped, when people were no longer interested either in politics or religion and there was once again a strong mandarinate to keep the literacy lid on, there was a new factor. Two new factors. A national literary industry looking for ways to diversify and a national literacy market yearning for diversion.

Naturally the government and the NGO's did their level best to cram everything back into the old pint pots but from 1660 until ... Walpole, they were obsessing over whether they wanted the status quo, the status quo ante or the status quo ante before that. Handing over power peaceably may be the gentlemanly way of doing things but it is not nearly as effective for settling matters as bloodletting. While the top people were at their oligarchical musings, the pot was bubbling away, lidless. But would it last? Many a slip 'twixt pot and lip. Still, **the fifth brick in the wall of exponential development had been laid.**

*   *   *

One more to go. It is not only top people who hate change, everybody hates change. In these days of exponential change, people can at least choose to be first-adopters, but what about the *first* first-adopters? The people that had to face exponential change for the first time in human history? How did matters appear to those world first-adopters, the English of the seventeenth, eighteenth and (will it never end?) the nineteenth century? How did the English turn a transitory set of highly peculiar circumstances into exponential development whether they wanted to or not? It was all very accidental, all very British.

The Stuarts favoured and intermittently tried to impose the Continental model of absolute monarchy, a system inimical to development, but Jacobite and Carolingian English Baroque was not popular and it was replaced by a popular regime, a system inimical to development, during the period 1642–60. Popular proved not to be popular and the experiment was halted in 1660. The English had had a double vaccination against the New Ways of Renaissance and Reformation, and turned with relief to an updated version of their tried and tested Plantagenet/Tudor model. This basically meant leaving most things to be decided at the local level by small landowners (Tories) and leaving anything requiring national attention to large landowners (Whigs). Works a treat. As long as you are an island nation, where not much requires national attention. If you are a continental nation and the centre has to hold, and hold everything, if you want to continue to be a continental nation, you will assuredly be a less happy land.

But over in England (even more truly an island nation now the damned Scots had been brought to heel) there was that added complication of a nation seething with literate dissenting ironmongers. Since both mass literacy and mass dissent were here to stay, could there be an England in which these people were guaranteed a place but knew their place? Probably. England is not hidebound when it comes to social hierarchies. It also has the good sense to retain social hierarchies, one wouldn't want to be Australia. That was not the problem. The problem was there was nothing to stop these educated (though never by universities) lower order innovators churning out better and better steam engines. This was deeply upsetting to all orders of society and something really ought to be done about it. But what? *Why* were they churning them out? It is not enough to be allowed to create an Industrial Revolution, you actually have to do it.

It was all because of that throwaway parenthetical remark 'educated (though never by universities)'. This is what is new, this is what distinguishes Newton from Newcomen, this is what distinguishes England from Sumer. Newton might have had to leave university to make something of himself but Newcomen *was not allowed to go to university in the first place*. Until the mid-nineteenth century Protestant dissenters were not permitted inside the hallowed halls. It is very old hat coming up with theories linking Protestantism with commercial enterprise but lots of places had Protestants, only one triggered exponential industrial enterprise. England was the only place where Protestants were allowed, but not allowed to go to university. But then again every civilisation since Sumer had prevented people, quite intelligent people, from going to university, England was first out of the traps with people who weren't allowed to go to university *but still got educated*. As soon as there were cheap books on every conceivable subject, everyman could stay at home and do a Newton.

These new non-educated educated people actually had an inbuilt advantage over Newton – ironmongers do not have their heads in the stars, Baptists do not spend half their working lives researching crackpot mysticism, their crackpot mysticism comes already installed. They are not subject to *any* of the attractions so carefully laid out by the academy to ensnare enquiring minds and turn them into unenquiring

156

minds. True, unenquiring minds are, broadly speaking, more useful to society but the point is one cannot go to university *and* invent the Industrial Revolution. Nobody knows why this is, it is just the way the human brain works. If the head is too full of information put there by authority figures in formal settings, the human brain can never get out from under. North Korea is everywhere.

It is still as true today as it was in the seventeenth century – or for that matter in the fourth millennium BC. The Industrial Revolution finished when the Wright Brothers got off the ground and our own Revolution – the non-physical one of the Information Age – is still dependent at every turn on people who, for one reason or another, managed to get out of university and into their garages just in time. Before the heady autodidacticism of *Practical Mechanics* got fatally derailed by the much easier catechism of celestial mechanics. Once you're told something you can never discover it.

*   *   *

So, to sum up human history. If you want to get ahead in the inventing game the cardinal rule is to avoid cardinal rule. Strong mandarinates always keep a lid on things, Calvinist, Catholic or Confucian. On the other hand, if you don't have a strong mandarinate you tend to get taken over by other people who do have strong mandarinates so you'll end up with a strong mandarinate anyway. It was a race against time! Would the English on their relatively secure island manage to quell their mandarinate long enough to be inventive and then use the inventions to keep out the other mandarinates long enough for the inventions to supply sufficient gewgaws to provide so much happiness they would never be tempted to return to strong mandarinates and would they then use the inventions to impose their own weak-mandarinate model on everyone else, thus solving the problem forever and ever amen? Yes.

END

INDEX

land surveyor 39
linguist 39
mentioned in charters 4, 10, 15, 19
'monastery name' 40, 44
missionary 39
remarkableness 39, 40
scholars of 7
Augustine St, of Hippo 40, 44, 45
Augustinians, order 66
Australia 156
authenticity
    authenticators 5, 11, 14-5
    land charters 14-5, 19-20, 21, 25
    Laws of Aethelbert 34
    relics 13
autodidacticism 157
Aylton 115

Babylo-Assyrian 35
Babylon 131, 141
Baptist 46, 150, 152, 156
bards 146-7
Baroque 152, 155
Bartholomew, arm only 13
Basque 137
Bayeux
    Bayeux Tapestry 12-13, 63-4
    Bishop of 17-9, 75
    distant from Canterbury 12
Becketomania 13
Bede, Venerable
    body in cathedral 77
    career 72, 73
    Holy Trinity of sources 46-7
    not saint 77
    source for Augustine 5-8, 36
    source for Caedmon 37-8
    source for Cuthbert 71-2, 77

Belgium 53, 72
Benedict XVI, pope 3
Benedict Biscop 73
Benedictine, order
    largest 19
    'monastery name' 40
    operate Echternach 90
    operate thirty British sites 87
    replace monks 75
    spread gospel book techniques 88
    Thomas Cook of their day 86-7
Benelux 91
Beowulf 35-6
Bermondsey 118
Bible
    exegetics 93
    High German 150
    Latin 24, 144
    not cheap 45, 149
    unBiblical 4
Bibliothèque nationale 51, 86
big picture 132
Big Thing 1
bishopric
    Bayeux 17-18
    Canterbury 3, 18-19, 21, 39
    Durham 75-6, 94-5
    Hereford 112-4, 129
    Irish 66
    Lindisfarne 94
    Llandaff 106-7
    Llandeilo 109
    Rochester 20-2, 39
    St David's 104
    Utrecht 91
Blaise, head of 13, 42-3
Blue Sky Rules 43
Bobbio 117

173

occupied by Romans 137
polis 154
potential for development
   140
Septimania 145
superior civilisation 143
Gregory I (the Great), pope
   defends art 11
   finger of 13
   historical source 48-9
   sends books 3, 5-6, 7, 13
Gregory VII (Hildebrand), pope 18
Grethi 111
Griffin, king 114
Guardian, The 1
Gueleran, bishop 20
guilds 152
Guinness Book of Records 37, 76,
   101, 129
Gundulph, bishop 21
Gutenberg, Johannes 92
Guthfrith, king 94
Guthred, king 79-80

Habsburgs 151
Halfdene (Halfdan Ragnarsson)
   78, 79
Haliwerfolc 94
Hamel, de [*see* de Hamel]
Han (Chinese) 140
Hanging Gardens 131, 141, 143
Harper, M J ii, 60
Heaney, Seamus 36
Hebrew 62, 138, 145
hedgerows 124
heere 125
helots 140
Henry II, king 110, 115
Henry IV, emperor 18

Hereford
   archaeology [*see* archaeology]
   attacked 127, 128
   Christianity 126, 129, 130
   city walls 128
   diocese 104, 112, 129
   earliest city in Europe 129
   meaning of name 125
   near Lichfield 112
   origins 126, 129
   saints 130
   SAS 128
   shire 124, 130
Hereford Cathedral
   antecedents 113, 129
   archaeology 129-30
   built in stone 114
   destruction 114
   Hereford Gospels 112, 114
   historians' source 114, 128
   landowner 116
   Library 111, 114
   Mappa Mundi 112
   re-founded in 7th century 113
   re-founded in 9th century 113
   re-founded in 11th century 114
   re-re-founded in 11th century
      114
Hereford Gospels 112-30
   Hereford Cathedral 116
   land charters 112-5
   little interest to historians 112
   palimpsest 116-7, 123
   provenance 112-4
   survives Welsh 114
Heritage Lottery 129
hermit 41, 78
Hero of Alexandria 152
Herodotus 37, 38
Hiberno-Norman 67
Hiberno-Saxon 84, 88

Hilda, abbess 37, 38
historians [*also see* history]
  abhor big picture 132
  Anglo-Saxon 15, 33-5, 134
  art historians 93
  bardic genealogies 146-7
  believe English is Anglo-Saxon
    26-8, 33
  brought up on Classics 140
  'careful ignoral' 97
  confuse Augustines 40
  credulity 14-5, 19, 23
  do not understand language
    58
  domain 131
  'either-or' technique 6, 7
  flinty-eyed 8
  follow the sources 27, 71, 138
  Ireland's contribution 57
  Irish 53, 54, 58
  land charters 87
  manuscript scholars 87, 99
  must not make it up 27
  need to believe charters 14-15
  professional 15, 28
  revisionist 64, 112
  Rochester's official 22
  Scottish 134-5
  self-effacing 27-8
  take things as found 27-8
  tools 131
  view of history 88
  vis-a-vis archaeologists 123,
    128, 131
  Welsh 99
history
  [*see also* historians]
    see also under
      Anglo-Saxon 27, 97, 123, 126
      English 8, 30, 97, 153-4
      Ireland 53-7, 65-9, 97, 103

      Wales 99-102
      Scotland 134-5
      Europe 143-4, 150-1
  absence 124
  and civilisation 131
  begins with writing 131
  bogus before 1300 AD 1, 117
  decides 140
  defined 131
  doubtful preferred to none 9
  heritage 75
  historical record 7, 14, 18,
    26-8, 35, 37, 53, 75-6, 77,
    82-3, 99, 106, 128, 131, 132,
    137-8, 147
  historiography 64, 102
  land tenure 16-17
  middling to good 88
  political before academic 27
  revisionist 64, 112
  tide reverses 83, 84, 92
  trade 9, 71
  upward story of 131
  world 30, 58, 83, 131-157
History of Britain Revealed, The ii
Hitler's Diaries 3
Hoe St, London E17 141-2
hoi polloi 139, 146
Holy Island 72
Holy Roman Empire 90
hoplite 143
horse
  and cart 132
  cavalry 143
  exchanged for gospel book 111
  stirrup 143
human condition 9
Hungary 53
hwyl 102
hydrology 141
hypothesis 82

177

first recorded 67-8, 101
incompatible with Latin 68
literary language 58, 67-8, 101
member, Goidelic branch 68, 69
unfamiliar to historians 58
Irish manuscript hound 63
Irish Pale 65-7
Irish Sea 76, 79
Irmina of Oeren 91
ironmongers 152, 156
Israel 138
Italy
    alphabet 135, 149
    annals 53
    Augustine's birthplace 30
    Bobbio 117
    Gospel of St Augustine 13, 15
    leather goods capital 117
    Odo's expedition 18
    precursors of Italian 135, 149
    Standard Italian 135, 149
    uncial script 9, 84
Ivar the Boneless 78

Jacobite 155
Jarrow [*see* Monkwearmouth]
Jerusalem 44
Jesus 46, 54, 64, 86
John, Gospel of 13
John the Baptist 46
Justice Cocklecarrot 20
Justus, St 20

Kells, book of [*see* Book of Kells]
Kells monastery
    becomes parish church 66
    book owned by 58
    book present at 52, 61
    book stolen from 54, 62

cusp of Pale 65-6
ecclesiastics 66
Echtgal, doorkeeper 61
land charters 64
land owned 59, 66
non-existence 66
refuge c 800 AD 52
Synod of Kells 66
Ua Breslen, priest 61
Kells (town)
    garrison established 66
    on cusp of Pale 65
    site of many battles 67
Kent 26, 28-30, 60, 99
Kilian, St 54
kine 58
King James (Bible) 85
know/known/knowledge
    academic, non-academic 82,
        141
    acknowledged by academics 32
    anachronisms 12
    autodidactic 157
    basic assumptions
        (paradigms) 82
    brain 133-4, 157
    'careful ignoral' 31-2
    circularity 106
    common sense 135, 136
    contemporary documents 27
    default assumption 28
    discredited 8
    ex hypothesi 151
    first academic hypotheses 82
    from authority 157
    from copies 14, 22, 25
    from other disciplines 33
    inferred 109
    invention 101
    jargon 152
    knowledge, elite 144

knowledge, practical 156-7
known known 138
known unknown 138
'nothing known' 28, 82
observational error 31-2
Occam's Razor 98
paradigm crash 36
scientific method 1, 31-2
unfalsifiable proposition 35
'what is known' 7
Kuhn, Thomas 36

lacuna 108
Lady Godiva 115, 116
Lake District 79
Lallan Scots 134
land charters
    Angevin 17, 64
    Anglo-Saxon 14-5, 17, 19, 21,
        24, 25, 101
    authenticity 14-15, 19, 23-4
    Book of Kells 50, 58-60, 61-2,
        66, 67, 99, 113
    Book of Llandaff 104
    Church uses 17, 19, 144
    court proceedings 20
    fabrication 19, 25, 94
    Gospels of St Augustine 13,
        15, 21, 25, 50, 59-60, 67, 99,
        113
    Ireland 64-5, 68
    Hereford Gospels 112-3, 114-6
    historical source 14, 50, 58-9, 99
    language in 24-5, 50, 67-8, 101,
        141
    Lichfield Gospels 99, 100-1,
        104, 110-11, 113
    Llandeilo 100-1, 104, 110-11
    Plumstead 17, 20
    Rochester 20-22, 24-5
    Wales 102-3, 104

land holdings
    Anglo-Saxon 16
    Ireland 65
    Llandeilo 106
    Norman 16
    Rochester 20
    St Augustine's Abbey 13
    Thurkill family 115
    Wales 101-3, 106
Land Registry 103, 143
land tenure, history of
    England 15-18
    Ireland 64
    Wales 101-3
language
    academese as meta-language 6
    artificial 138
    cannot be written 132, 133
    chief diversion 133
    cognates 134
    demotic [*see* main entry]
    Indo-European 68
    infinite sounds 133, 135, 136
    limited palette now 133
    literary 26-7, 67, 134, 135, 144,
        147
    natural 29-30, 133-6, 146, 148,
        149
    phonetic 29-30
    proto- 69
    related 134
    Romance 137
    second 139
    'speak as you write' 133
    the old switcheroo 138
    'word-formulations' 132, 133,
        134, 135, 144
    written languages
        Anglo-Saxon [*see* main entry]
        Arabic 138, 145
        Babylo-Assyrian 35

179

called in by Privy Council 38-9
copies 30, 53
defined 4
earliest with English writing
        4, 23
entire Irish corpus 56, 57
expensive 92, 144, 149
forgeries 1, 50
Hereford 97
Hiberno-Saxon 84
hundreds of Brendans 56
illustrated 11, 55, 57, 70, 97, 112
Insular 88
Irish 56, 57, 59, 61, 67, 68
Irish manuscript hound 63
missing pages 11, 62-3
normal wear and tear 11, 62
not expensive 92-3
not scientifically dated 2
palimpsests 117-8, 123
precious objects 56, 63
production 118-23
Proust's 51
role in civilisation 131
same author 87-8
same tradition 112
specialists 2, 87, 99, 118
survival 22, 37-8, 55
too complete provenance 72
tourist brochures 86
world firsts 23, 100, 101
world's most remarkable 4
Manuscript A.II.10 86, 92-3
created c 700 AD 92-3
fragment only 92-3
not gospel book 92-3
owned by Durham Cathedral
        92-3
uses of 92-3
work product 92-3
Manx 68

Mappa Mundi 112
marcher lords 96
Marge 12, 100
marginalia
        Book of Kells 50, 58, 59
        defined 9
        earlier Irish books 68
        Gospels of St Augustine 9-10,
                13, 58
        land charters 10, 13, 50, 58
        Lichfield Gospels 104, 101
        terminus ante quem 9-10, 58
Marienbad 36
Marius, Gaius 154
Mark, Gospel of 4, 10, 13
martyrologies 154
Mary, St (Virgin Mary)
        impregnated 31
        Madonna and child art 64
        mispronounced by Welsh 106
Matilda, empress 16-17
Matthew, Gospel of 11, 13, 62
Meath 52, 58, 60, 67
medieval 13-14, 22, 51, 57, 95-6,
        108-9
Mediterranean 135
Medway Council Archives 24
Medway Studies Centre 30
*Meetings with Remarkable
        Manuscripts* 1
Megalithic Empire, The ii
Megalithic Trade Route, A ii
Memoranda 111
Mercia 29, 98, 100-1, 115, 126, 129
Mercury 31-2, 33
Merovingian 89
Mesopotamia 83-4, 100, 131
metallurgy 83, 141, 150
Methodists 130
Middle Ages 91, 95, 148, 149, 150
Milfrid, nobleman 113

187

Lightning Source UK Ltd.
Milton Keynes UK
UKHW020152201118
332613UK00009B/271/P

9 780954 291129